Brace Brace

Oli Forsyth

GW00692035

methuen | drama

LONDON • NEW YORK • OXFORD • NEW DELHI • SYDNEY

METHUEN DRAMA
Bloomsbury Publishing Plc
50 Bedford Square, London, WC1B 3DP, UK
1385 Broadway, New York, NY 10018, USA
29 Earlsfort Terrace, Dublin 2, Ireland

BLOOMSBURY, METHUEN DRAMA and the Methuen
Drama logo are trademarks of Bloomsbury Publishing Plc

First published in Great Britain 2024

Copyright © Oli Forsyth, 2024

Oli Forsyth has asserted his right under the Copyright, Designs
and Patents Act, 1988, to be identified as author of this work.

For legal purposes the Acknowledgements on p. vii
constitute an extension of this copyright page.

Cover design by Jade Barnett

Cover artwork by Guy Sanders

All rights reserved. No part of this publication may be reproduced or
transmitted in any form or by any means, electronic or mechanical, including
photocopying, recording, or any information storage or retrieval system,
without prior permission in writing from the publishers.

Bloomsbury Publishing Plc does not have any control over, or responsibility
for, any third-party websites referred to or in this book. All internet addresses
given in this book were correct at the time of going to press. The author and
publisher regret any inconvenience caused if addresses have changed or sites
have ceased to exist, but can accept no responsibility for any such changes.

No rights in incidental music or songs contained in the work are hereby
granted and performance rights for any performance/presentation
whatsoever must be obtained from the respective copyright owners.

All rights whatsoever in this play are strictly reserved and application
for performance etc. should be made before rehearsals to Julia Tyrrell
Management Ltd of 57 Greenham Road, London, N10 1LN, UK.
No performance may be given unless a licence has been obtained.
No rights in incidental music or songs contained in the
Work are hereby granted and performance rights for any
performance/presentation whatsoever must be obtained
from the respective copyright owners.

A catalogue record for this book is available from the British Library.

A catalog record for this book is available from the Library of Congress.

ISBN: PB: 978-1-3505-3445-2
ePDF: 978-1-3505-3447-6
eBook: 978-1-3505-3446-9

Series: Modern Plays

Typeset by Mark Heslington Ltd, Scarborough, North Yorkshire
Printed and bound in Great Britain

To find out more about our authors and books visit
www.bloomsbury.com and sign up for our newsletters.

THE ROYAL COURT THEATRE
PRESENTS

BRACE BRACE

By Oli Forsyth

BRACE BRACE was first performed at The Royal Court Jerwood
Theatre Upstairs, Sloane Square, on Thursday 3 October 2024.

BRACE BRACE
By Oli Forsyth

Cast (in alphabetical order):

Ray Phil Dunster
The Man Craige Els
Sylvia Anjana Vasan

Director Daniel Raggett
Designer Anna Reid
Lighting Designer Simeon Miller
Sound Designer Paul Arditti
Casting Director Arthur Carrington
Fight Director Alex Payne
Stage Manager Lavinia Serban
Deputy Stage Manager Lizzie Cooper
Set built by Royal Court Stage Department & Ridiculous Solutions

From the Royal Court, on this production:

Lead Producer Hannah Lyall
Sound Supervisor David McSeveney
Lighting Programmer Lucinda Plummer
Costume Supervisor Katie Price
Production Manager Marius Rønning
Lighting Supervisor Daisy Simmons
Company Manager Mica Taylor

Oli is this year's recipient of the Jerwood New Playwright accolade. He is also the recipient of the inaugural Davidson PlayGC Bursary, supported by PlayGC Theatre Company and the Alan Davidson Foundation.

The Royal Court Theatre's Jerwood New Playwright Programme is supported by Jerwood Foundation.

Recipient of The Davidson PlayGC Bursary, supported by PlayGC Theatre Company and the Alan Davidson Foundation.

Presented in partnership with Mark Gordon Pictures.

Oli Forsyth (Writer)

Theatre includes: The Pox, One Taken One Left, Cash Cow (Hampstead); Such Filthy F*cks (Pleasance/Vault); Cornermen (& Old Red Lion/ Pleasance/Vault/New Diorama), Happy Dave (& New Diorama), Kings (& New Diorama), Tinderbox (Smoke & Oakum).

Paul Arditti (Sound Designer)

For the Royal Court: Paul was Head of Sound at the Royal Court from 1993 to 2001, designing over 70 productions including Jumpy, Plasticine, 4:48 Psychosis, Far Away, Blasted, Via Dolorosa, The Weir, Mojo, Shopping and Fucking, The Kitchen, Some Voices, and Hysteria.

Paul is currently an Associate at the National.

Theatre for the National includes: The Odyssey Part 5: The Underworld, The Motive And The Cue (& West End), Our Generation (& Chichester), Jack Absolute Flies Again, Dick Wittington, Rutherford and Son, Absolute Hell, Pericles, Macbeth, Amadeus, Beginning, Mosquitoes, The Threepenny Opera, Ma Rainey's Black Bottom, wonder.land, Everyman, The Hard Problem, Behind the Beautiful Forevers, King Lear, Edward II, London Road, Collaborators, One Man Two Guvnors (& West End/Broadway), Saint Joan, The Pillowman (& Broadway).

Other theatre includes: Stranger Things: The First Shadow (West End); Guys and Dolls, The Book of Dust: La Belle Sauvage, A Midsummer Night's Dream and Julius Caesar (Bridge); The Jungle (National/Young Vic/West End/New York/San Francisco).

Awards include: Tony, Drama Desk and Olivier awards for Billy Elliot the Musical in the West End and on Broadway; an Olivier Nomination for The Inheritance; Tony nominations for Mary Stuart and The Inheritance; an Evening Standard Award for Festen in the West End; a Drama Desk Award for The Pillowman on Broadway.

Paul announced his retirement in 2024, so BRACE BRACE is probably his final sound design.

Arthur Carrington (Casting Director)

As Casting Director, for the Royal Court: Bluets, Mates in Chelsea, Blue Mist, Hope has a Happy Meal, Black Superhero, Graceland, Jews. In Their Own Words, That Is Not Who I Am, two Palestinians go dogging, The Glow, A Fight Against... (Una Lucha Contra...), Maryland, Poet in da Corner.

As Casting Director, other theatre includes: Little Deaths (Summerhall); Visit from an Unknown Woman (Hampstead); Liberation Squares (Nottingham Playhouse/Fifth Word); The Contingency Plan (Sheffield Crucible); Barefoot in the Park (Pitlochry Festival/Royal Lyceum); Returning to Haifa (Finborough); The Ugly One (Park); The Mountaintop (Young Vic).

As Casting Associate, for the Royal Court, theatre includes: The Ferryman (& West End/Broadway), Hangmen (& West End / US tour) and over 40 further productions.

As Casting Associate, other theatre includes: Slave Play, The Hills of California, Lyonesse, The Pillowman, Hamnet (& RSC); Jerusalem, Leopoldstadt, Uncle Vanya, The Night of the Iguana, Rosmersholm, True West (West End); Macbeth (UK/US Tour); La Cage Aux Folles (Regent's Park Open Air); Drive Your Plow Over the Bones of the Dead (Complicité/Tour); Shipwreck, Albion (Almeida); A Very, Very, Very Dark Matter (Bridge).

Film includes: The Unlikely Pilgrimage of Harold Fry, Maryland, Ballywater.

Lizzie Cooper (Deputy Stage Manager)

As Deputy Stage Manager theatre includes: Kyoto (RSC); Nachtland (Young Vic); Lyonesse, Leopoldstadt, J'Ouvert, Pinter at the Pinter Season, Jeruselam (West End); Spitting Image: Live (Birmingham Rep).

As Assistant Stage Manager, theatre includes: Rutherford & Son, The Red Barn (National); The Lorax (The Old Vic & Royal Alexandra); Hamlet, The Maids, Harry Potter and the Cursed Child, Girl from the North Country (West End); The Merchant of Venice, Carmen Disruption (Almeida).

As Stage Manager, theatre includes: The Pitchfork Disney & Killer (Shoreditch Town Hall).

Phil Dunster (Ray)

Theatre includes: Oklahoma in Concert, The Entertainer (West End); Pink Mist (Bush/Bristol Old Vic); Much Ado About Nothing (RBL).

Television includes: Ted Lasso, Surface, The Devil's Hour, Dracula, The Trouble with Maggie Cole, Catherine the Great, No Offence, Humans, Strike Back, Save Me, Man in an Orange Shirt, Catastrophe, Stan Lee's Lucky Man.

Film includes: The Good Liar, Judy, All is True, Murder on the Orient Express, Megan Leavey, The Rise and Fall of the Krays.

Craige Els (The Man)

Theatre includes: Just for One Day (Jamie Wilson Productions/Old Vic); Chess in Concert (Theatre Royal Drury Lane); Matilda the Musical (RSC/West End/UK Tour); That Day We Sang (Royal Exchange); Timon of Athens, Antigone, The Kitchen, The Cherry Orchard, Blood and Gifts (National); 65 Miles (Paines Plough); Once Upon a Time in Wigan (Hull Truck).

Television includes: Blood of My Blood, Coma, The Responder, G'wed, Fool Me Once, Dr Who, Sliced, Coronation Street, Hailmakers, Ripper Street, Chickens, The Bletchley Circle, Law and Order, Call the Midwife, Endeavour.

Film includes: RIPD: Rise of the Damned, The Imitation Game, Leave to Remain, Anna Karenina, Never Forget.

Audio includes: Home Front, Proud, Absent, Lennon: A Week in the Life, Exam-Slam.

Simeon Miller (Lighting Designer)

For the Royal Court: Cowbois (& RSC).

Other theatre includes: Pass It On, As We Face The Sun (Bush); Alice In Wonderland (Liverpool Everyman/Plymouth Theatre Royal); The Sun Shines For Everyone, The Mob Reformers (Lyric Hammersmith); The Book of Will (& Queen's, Hornchurch/Shakespeare North Playhouse), An Adventure (Bolton Octagon); Ruckus (Southwark Playhouse/Summerhall Edinburgh); Jekyll and Hyde (Derby/Queen's, Hornchurch); Christmas in the Sunshine (Unicorn); Follow the Signs (Soho); The Poison Belt (Jermyn Street); Project Dictator (New Diorama); Metamorphoses (Shakespeare's Globe); Subject Mater (Edinburgh Fringe); Black Holes (International tour); High Rise State of Mind (UK tour).

Alex Payne (Fight Director)

Theatre includes: Opening Night, An Enemy of the People (West End); Saxon Court, A Lie of The Mind (Southwark Playhouse); A Sherlock Christmas Carol (Marylebone).

As Associate Fight Director, theatre includes: Macbeth (Dock X/Shakespeare Theatre Company); The Grapes of Wrath (National); Fawlty Towers - The Play (West End).

Live performance includes: Rumble in the Jungle (Rematch Live); Lights Camera Action, Celebration of Superhero's (Warner Bros Abu Dhabi); Bridgerton, Star Wars, Stranger Things (Secret Cinema).

Opera includes: Il Tabaro (ROH); The Magic Flute (Nevill Holt).

Stunt Performance work includes: Vikings, Mary Queen of Scots, Taboo, Vikings: Valhalla.

Daniel Raggett (Director)

As director, theatre includes: Accidental Death of an Anarchist (Sheffield Theatres/Lyric Hammersmith/Theatre Royal Haymarket); ANNA X (West End); The Vortex (Chichester Festival); The Human Voice (Gate).

As associate director, theatre includes: West Side Story (Broadway); Network (National & Belasco Theatre).

Film Credits include: Hermit (Short).

Anna Reid (Designer)

For the Royal Court: For Black Boys Who Have Considered Suicide When the Hue Gets Too Heavy (Nouveau Riche/Boundless/New Diorama/West End).

Theatre includes: The Memory Of Water, Sleepwalking, Cash Cow, Paradise, The Hoes (Hampstead); Sessions (Paines Plough/Soho); Dust (New York Theatre Workshop/Soho); Four Minutes Twelve Seconds, The Kitchen Sink, Jumpers For Goalposts (Oldham Coliseum); Late Night Staring At High Res Pixels, Scrounger, I'm Gonna Pray For You So Hard (Finborough); The Sweet Science Of Bruising (Wilton's Music Hall); Our Country's Good, A Midsummer Night's Dream (Tobacco Factory); Twelfth Night, Collective Rage, Dear Brutus, The Cardinal, School Play (Southwark); Soft Animals, Fury (Soho); Mary's Babies, Dry Land (Jermyn Street); Rasheeda Speaking (Trafalgar Studios); Schism (Park); Grotty (Bunker); Tiny Dynamite (Old Red Lion); Rattle Snake (Live, Newcastle/Theatre Royal, York/Soho); Sex Worker's Opera [set design] (Compagnietheater, Amsterdam/ National tour); Arthur's World (Bush); Hippolytos (V&A Museum); Hamlet (Riverside Studios).

Opera includes: Opera Double Bill - Judith Weir's Miss Fortune and Menotti's The Telephone (Guildhall).

Anna was selected to represent the UK as an emerging designer at World Stage Design in Taipei.

Lavinia Serban (Stage Manager)

As Company Manager, other theatre includes: SIX The Musical (Tour); The Trials (Donmar).

As Deputy Stage Manager, theatre includes: Eddie Izzard's Hamlet (Riverside Studios); Watch on the Rhine (Donmar); The Secretaries (Young Vic).

As Props Supervisor, theatre includes: Gods of the Game (Grange Park Opera).

Anjana Vasan (Sylvia)

Theatre includes: A Streetcar Named Desire (Almeida/Phoenix), Summer and Smoke (Almeida/Duke of York's); A Doll's House (Lyric Hammersmith); Rutherford and Son, Dara, Behind the Beautiful Forevers (National); An Adventure (Bush); King Lear, Midsummer Night's Dream (Globe); Life of Galileo (Young Vic); Image of an Unknown Young Woman (Gate); Macbeth (Park Armory New York/ Broadway); Taming of the Shew, Much Ado About Nothing (RSC).

Television includes: Towards Zero, Black Mirror, Killing Eve, We Are Lady Parts, Sex Education, Hang Ups, Fresh Meat.

Film includes: Wicked Little Letters, Cyrano, Mogul Mowgli.

Awards include: Evening Standard Theatre Award for Best Actress (A Streetcar Named Desire); Laurence Olivier Award for Best Actress in a Supporting Role (A Streetcar Names Desire); RTS Award for Best Female Comedy Performance (We Are Lady Parts).

THE ROYAL COURT THEATRE

The Royal Court Theatre is the writers' theatre. It is a leading force in world theatre for cultivating and supporting writers - undiscovered, emerging and established.

Since 1956, we have commissioned and produced hundreds of writers, from John Osborne to Mohamed-Zain Dada. Royal Court plays from every decade are now performed on stages and taught in classrooms and universities across the globe.

Through the writers, the Royal Court is at the forefront of creating restless, alert, provocative theatre about now. We open our doors to the unheard voices and free thinkers that, through their writing, change our way of seeing.

We strive to create an environment in which differing voices and opinions can co-exist. In current times, it is becoming increasingly difficult for writers to write what they want or need to write without fear, and we will do everything we can to rise above a narrowing of viewpoints.

Through all our work, we strive to inspire audiences and influence future writers with radical thinking and provocative discussion.

🐦 royalcourt 📘 royalcourttheatre

Supported using public funding by
**ARTS COUNCIL
ENGLAND**

ROYAL COURT SUPPORTERS

Our incredible community of supporters makes it possible for us to achieve our mission of nurturing and platforming writers at every stage of their careers. Our supporters are part of our essential fabric – they help to give us the freedom to take bigger and bolder risks in our work, develop and empower new voices, and create world-class theatre that challenges and disrupts the theatre ecology.

To all our supporters, thank you. You help us to write the future.

PUBLIC FUNDING

CHARITABLE PARTNERS

BackstageTrust

COCKAYNE

T. S. ELIOT FOUNDATION

JERWOOD FOUNDATION

CORPORATE SPONSORS & SUPPORTERS

Aqua Financial Ltd
Cadogan
Concord Theatricals
Edwardian Hotels, London
Sustainable Wine Solutions
Walpole

CORPORATE MEMBERS

Bloomberg Philanthopies
Sloane Stanley

TRUSTS & FOUNDATIONS

Maria Björnson Memorial Fund
Martin Bowley Charitable Trust
Chalk Cliff Trust
The Noël Coward Foundation
Cowley Charitable Foundation
The Davidson Play GC Bursary
The Lynne Gagliano Writers' Award
Theatres Trust
The Harold Hyam Wingate Foundation
John Lyon's Charity
The Marlow Trust
Clare McIntyre's Bursary
Old Possum's Practical Trust
Richard Radcliffe Charitable Trust
Rose Foundation
Royal Victoria Hall Foundation
The Thistle Trust
The Thompson Family Charitable Trust

PRESS NIGHT PARTNER

Prime Time

INDIVIDUAL SUPPORTERS

Artistic Director's Circle

Katie Bradford
Jeremy & Becky Broome
Clyde Cooper
Debbie De Girolamo &
Ben Babcock
Denzil Fernandez
Dominique & Neal Gandhi
Lydia & Manfred Gorvy
David & Jean Grier
Charles Holloway OBE
Linda Keenan
Andrew & Ariana Rodger
Jack Thorne & Rachel Mason
Sandra Treagus for
ATA Assoc. LTD
Anonymous

Writers' Circle

Chris & Alison Cabot
Cas Donald
Robyn Durie
Héloïse & Duncan Matthews KC
Emma O'Donoghue
Maureen & Tony Wheeler
Anonymous

Directors' Circle

Piers Butler
Fiona Clements
Professor John Collinge
Julian & Ana Garel-Jones
Carol Hall
Dr Timothy Hyde
Anonymous

Platinum Members

Moira Andreae
Tyler Bollier
Katie Bullivant
Anthony Burton CBE
Matthew Dean
Emily Fletcher
Beverley Gee
Damien Hyland
Susanne Kapoor
David P Kaskel &
Christopher A Teano
Peter & Maria Kellner
Robert Ledger &
Sally Moulsdale
Frances Lynn
Mrs Janet Martin
Andrew McIver
Brian & Meredith Niles
Corinne Rooney
Anita Scott
Bhags Sharma
Dr Wendy Sigle
Brian Smith
Mrs Caroline Thomas
Sir Robert & Lady Wilson
Anonymous

With thanks to our Silver and Gold Supporters, and our Friends and Good Friends, whose support we greatly appreciate.

Royal Court Theatre
Sloane Square,
London SW1W 8AS
Tel: 020 7565 5050
info@royalcourttheatre.com
www.royalcourttheatre.com

Artistic Director
David Byrne
Executive Director
Will Young

Associate Playwrights
**Mike Bartlett,
Ryan Calais Cameron,
Vinay Patel, Nina Segal.**
Associate Playwright &
Dramaturg
Gillian Greer
Associate Playwright
& Young Writer's
Associate
Beth Flintoff
Resident Director
Aneesha Srinivasan
Artistic Co-ordinator
Ailsa Dann

Head of Producing &
Partnerships
Steven Atkinson
Producers
**Hannah Lyall,
Ralph Thompson.**
Producing Co-ordinator
Winnie Imara
Assistant to the Artistic
& Executive Directors
Vanessa Ng

Director of
Development
Anuja Batra
Senior Development
Manager
Amy Millward
Development Officer
Nash Metaxas

Head of Production
Marius Rønning
Company Manager
Mica Taylor^
Head of Lighting
Deanna Towli
Deputy Head of Lighting
Lucinda Plummer
Lighting Technician
Daisy Simmons
Lighting Programmer
Lizzie Skellett
Head of Stage
Steve Evans
Deputy Head of Stage
Maddy Collins
Stage Show Technician
Oscar Sale
Head of Sound
David McSeveney
Deputy Head of Sound
Jet Sharp
Head of Costume
Lucy Walshaw
Deputy Head of
Costume
Katie Price

Director of Marketing &
Communications
Rachael Welsh
Marketing & Sales
Manager
Benjamin McDonald
Digital Content
Producer (Videography)
Giovanni Edwards
Marketing Officer
Elizabeth Carpenter
Press Officer
Ella Gold
Communications
Assistant
**Natasha Ryszka-
Onions**
Press & Publicity
Bread and Butter PR

Living Archive
Lead Researcher &
Project Co-ordinator
Sula Douglas-Folkes
Digital Research
Assistant
Amber Fraser

Finance Director
Helen Perryer
Finance Manager
Olivia Amory
Senior Finance &
Payroll Officer
Will Dry
Finance &
Administration
Assistant
Bukola Sonubi

Head of People
Olivia Shaw

General Manager
Rachel Dudley
Front of House Manager
**Jennelle Reece-
Gardner**
Senior Duty House
Manager
Ronay Poole
Duty House Manager/
Usher
**Emer Halton-O'Mahony,
James Wilson**
Box Office Sales
Assistants
**William Byam Shaw,
Ollie Harrington,
Felix Pilgrim.**
Box Office &
Administration
Assistant
Phoebe Coop
Stage Door Keepers
**James Graham,
Léa Jackson,
Paul Lovegrove.**

Head of Operations &
Sustainability
Robert Smael
Bar & Restaurant
Manager
Adam Turns
Bar & Floor Supervisors
**Val Farrow, Matthew
Paul, Lucy Stepan,
Milla Tikkanen.**
General Maintenance
Technician
David Brown

Thanks to all of our
Ushers and Bar &
Kitchen staff.

^ The post of
Company Manager
is supported by
Charles Holloway OBE

ENGLISH STAGE
COMPANY

President
**Dame Joan Plowright
CBE**

Honorary Council
**Graham Devlin CBE
Alan Grieve CBE
Martin Paisner CBE**

Council Chairman
Anthony Burton CBE
Members
**Jennette Arnold OBE
Noma Dumezweni
Neal Gandhi
Pamela Jikiemi
Mwenya
Kawesha Mark
Ravenhill
Andrew Rodger
Anita Scott
Lord Stewart Wood
Mahdi Yahya**

Let's be friends. With benefits.

Our Friends and Good Friends are part of the fabric of the Royal Court. They help us to create world-class theatre, and in return they receive early access to our shows and a range of exclusive benefits.

Join today and become a part of our community.

Become a Friend (from £40 a year)

Benefits include:

- Priority Booking
- Advanced access to £15 Monday tickets
- 10% Bar & Kitchen discount (including Court in the Square)
- 10% off Royal Court playtexts

Become a Good Friend (from £95 a year)

In addition to the Friend benefits, our Good Friends also receive:

- Five complimentary playtexts for Royal Court productions
- An invitation for two to step behind the scenes of the Royal Court Theatre at a special event

Our Good Friends' membership also includes a voluntary donation. This extra support goes directly towards supporting our work and future, both on and off stage.

To become a Friend or a Good Friend, or to find out more about the different ways in which you can get involved, visit our website: royalcourttheatre. com/support-us

The English Stage Company at the Royal Court Theatre is a registered charity (No. 231242)

Brace Brace

For Ella

'Eyes that light up, Eyes look through you.'

And, as always, for N.E.O.N.

My deepest thanks must go to Mike Bartlett, Joelle Brabban, Jack Bradfield, David Byrne, Daniel Goldman, Mark Gordon, Gillian Greer, Ed MacArthur, Will Mortimer, Luke Murphy, Dom O'Hanlon, Katie Pesskin, Stewart Pringle, Daniel Raggett, Julia Tyrrell, The Royal Court Theatre, Robert and Lisa Gordon Clark, Play GC Theatre and the Alan Davidson Foundation, Methuen Drama.

Characters

Sylvia
Ray
The Man, **Al**, **Sam**, **Interviewer** *(played by same actor)*

Notes

Three broad states of action exist:

In STATE 1 the actors talk with the audience and each other. They compete to tell the story, trying to win over audience members and correcting plot points. The lighting is broad and clear to bring the audience in. This state is set at the exact time of each performance.

STATE 2 focuses on one actor. In this state, they can speak to the audience without being heard by the other characters. These moments are usually short.

STATE 3 is that of a conventional scene. A fourth wall exists and the time and space of each scene is felt truly by the characters.

The transitions between the states should be seamless and not protracted. They should aid the rhythm of the dialogue.

Beats in ascending order of duration:

Micro beat

Quick Beat

Beat

Pause

Silence

– within a line indicates a change of thought.

– at the end of a line indicates an interruption.

. . . indicates a tailing off

[] indicates a word not spoken

Scene One

A clear stage.

In the dark, we hear the sound of an aeroplane's roaring engines, warning buzzers, shaking panels.

Sylvia *and* **Ray** *(thirties) enter from opposite sides.*

Sound cuts off. Lights up.

STATE 1.

Ray Right . . . let's try again.

Sylvia Shall I [start] . . .?

Ray Yep.

Sylvia Sure?

Ray All yours.

They speak out to the audience.

Sylvia The first time we met – (*Back to* **Ray**.) Is that . . .?

He mimes rushing through.

Sylvia Yeh, so, the first time we met was, uh, at a party.

Ray House party.

Sylvia I was – it was a friend of mine. But he was doing the whole –

Ray I wasn't doing anything.

Sylvia Sure, but you were . . .

Ray I was leaning against a fridge.

Sylvia Yes, but with, y'know . . . the antennae on.

Ray Can we . . . [Hurry this up]?

Sylvia Like a siren song for single women.

Ray You having just left the convent, of course –

Sylvia   I'm just saying, you were pretty clear –

Ray   The first time was at a house party and I thought she was the most striking person I'd ever met.

Sylvia   Thank you.

Ray   She walked right up to me, no names, and just started talking.

Sylvia   I was in a decisive phase –

Ray   Having just done a whole load of decision in the bathroom.

Sylvia   He was all on his own. I was being nice.

Ray   You were. Very nice.

They smile at each other. Quick beat.

Ray   Tell them your chat-up line –

Sylvia *covers her face.*

Sylvia   No. No, no, no –

Ray   Like a siren song for single men –

Sylvia   That's known as a 'callback' if anyone's –

Ray   What was your line –?

Sylvia   I was in a philosophical phase –

Ray   Tell them –

STATE 3.

We fly into the party. The lights get tighter.

Sylvia   I read something today about a study they've done –

Ray   Sorry, who's they?

Sylvia   A scientific . . . body.

Ray   I've heard of them.

Sylvia   And in this study, which is quite shocking, they dropped, like, 20,000 slices of buttered toast, right?

Ray   Right.

Sylvia   And of these thousands of drops – no, I'm being very serious here – they found the toast fell, butter side down . . . 66 per cent of the time.

Quick beat.

Ray   Wow.

Sylvia   That's high, right?

Ray   Two-thirds is quite high, yeh.

Sylvia   Which leaves them two possible conclusions. One: that the butter increases the weight. Or two . . .

Ray   Go on.

Sylvia   The world is just scientifically unfair.

Ray   Oh. Uh . . .

Quick beat. **Ray** *thinks.*

Ray   The second one. I think the world is unfair.

Sylvia   What?

Ray   Bad things happen, people are awful, and it's all very, very unfair.

Quick beat.

Sylvia   Christ.

Ray   Sorry.

Sylvia   You really feel that?

Ray   I think so.

Sylvia   Really?

Ray   Yeh.

Beat. **Sylvia** *gawps.*

Sylvia   I was – I was going to ask for your number.

Micro-beat. **Ray** *adjusts.*

Ray   Well, you can have it. I would *love* for you to –

Sylvia   Don't want it now.

Ray   Why not?

Sylvia   It's just such a negative view of people.

Ray (*thinking fast*)   Right, yeh. It is possible, though, that I was wrong. Or lying.

Sylvia   Lying?

Ray   Yeh, compulsive, can't help myself. It's honestly terrible.

Beat. **Sylvia** *stares, nods, smiles.*

Sylvia   I think you were.

Ray   You think I was what?

Sylvia   Lying.

Ray   I think I was too.

Sylvia   I just don't believe someone with a face as nice as yours could see the world in such a horrible way.

STATE 2.

Half the lighting snaps off, leaving **Ray** *smiling and talking to us.*

Ray   Listen, there's a really bad bit coming up, so, y'know, try and enjoy the nice moments while they're here, yeh?

STATE 1.

They both move freely.

Sylvia   I'm still mortified by that.

Ray   'A face as nice as yours'? Sign me up.

Sylvia When you know, you know.

Ray We had our first date the very next day.

Sylvia Had our first few things the very next day –

Ray Darling!

Sylvia Sweetheart.

Funny beat.

Ray It was an exciting time.

Sylvia Very exciting.

Ray When you meet someone new and you gain friends, trade families. You feel them expanding into your life. Filling it.

Sylvia Which can be –

Ray Some people hate it –

Sylvia But for us it was great –

Ray After one year –

Sylvia We enhanced each other.

Micro-beat. **Ray** *acknowledges the change.*

Sylvia Sorry –

Ray That's ok –

Sylvia I just wanted to say, we enhanced each other.

Ray We did. Shall we . . .?

Sylvia Yep.

Ray *gets back on the script. The change lingers with them both for a moment.*

Ray Ok. My dad *loved* her.

Sylvia Guilty.

Ray   Nearly fell off his chair when he found out I was
dating a: Digital. Campaigns. Manager.

Sylvia   Very easily impressed, your dad.

Ray   He thought it was subliminal messaging and dark
arts –

Sylvia   But really it's just about sensing what people might
be feeling –

Ray   Which is something you turned out to be very good at.

Sylvia   And I think it's really important to say –

Ray   Easy now –

Sylvia   No, but they might – some people hear advertising
and think nepotism. But I didn't know anyone. I had no
connections, nothing. All I had was –

Ray   An arts degree and the right accent.

Sylvia   Don't laugh at that – it's –

Ray   Her granddad was a plumber though, so you can all
relax. This is an authentic working-class story.

Sylvia   I never said that.

Ray   No. But it's the only way we could get a gig here.

Sylvia (*patient*)   Ray, this is exactly the kind of thing that
slows us down.

Ray   Yes, sorry. Your family were less thrilled by my
lifestyle –

Sylvia   Not true, they found you very interesting –

Ray   She always gets embarrassed by this. To be fair, I get
embarrassed by this.

Sylvia   He was working in, sort of, transgressive
performance art, based around –

Ray   I was trying to be a stand-up.

Sylvia Yeh, that was – yeh.

Ray You wouldn't think it. I know you wouldn't, but spent every penny I had trying to play places like this. Well, not quite like this . . . Wrong jokes, you see.

Sylvia 'You ever notice how guys drive like this?'

Ray That was *never* one of my – ignore her. This is slander –

Sylvia I always found him funny. Very funny –

Ray You have to say that –

Sylvia Just not on stage.

Ray Right, there we are.

Sylvia Initially he was great, really flying, but after a couple of years something shifted. It started sounding bitter –

Ray I was a bit late, maybe. My voice didn't fit with the . . . vibes, or –

Sylvia The act became angrier and nastier –

Ray And fundamentally not very funny. So that career crashed.

Sylvia (*kindly*) It didn't crash . . .

Ray Everyone was getting embarrassed, I felt like I didn't have anything to offer – which isn't to say that *any* of the rest of them do – But I – I decided to go. Screw 'em.

Sylvia Yeh.

Ray I sound calm now, but at the time . . .

Sylvia 'The liberals got me!' –

Ray I took it very badly. I was not in a good place –

Sylvia Which was unusual for him.

Ray   If you keep telling someone that their view of the world is – is contemptibly wrong – then you're likely to make that person a bit, y'know . . . volatile.

Sylvia   It's very strange watching someone you love becoming this different, paranoid person.

Ray   Is it?

Beat. **Sylvia** *nearly responds.*

Sylvia   But, you turned it around.

Ray   I did. PGC. New job. And I took up yoga.

Sylvia   Ever seen a grown man Crow Pose on a Tuesday morning?

Ray   She has.

Sylvia   I have.

Ray   So I sort myself out, she's racing up the greasy pole.

Sylvia   Stop it.

Ray   As we eased from some early hiccups into being painfully pleased with ourselves. Didn't we, darling?

Sylvia   So what do you do?

Both   You get married.

Ray   Never fancied it myself.

Sylvia   But I did.

Ray   And it was amazing.

Sylvia   Champagne, speeches, big party, and then . . .

Ray   Then the honeymoon.

Sylvia   Yeh.

Beat. **Ray** *sighs.*

Ray   Alright. Let's get to the bad part.

The energy changes as they go straight into:

Scene Two

Sylvia   So, the honeymoon.

Ray   Three weeks on a beach.

Sylvia   Just a small fortune and one twelve-hour flight away –

Ray   And she hates flying. So we're in the queue, all lovey and happy and smiley – you'd have hated us –

Sylvia   And there's two people behind us. A dad and a little girl, maybe seven.

Ray   Everyone else has run a mile, they're the only ones stupid enough to engage with us, so we get to chatting.

Sylvia   Where have you come from? Really? Us too! We probably took the same train!

Ray   Excruciating –

Sylvia   Turns out the child is the only one flying. Her mum manages a hotel out there and it's summer holidays.

Ray   I go to check the bag in, and by the time I come back –

STATE 3.

Ray   We're what?!

Sylvia   Keep your voice down!

Ray   How the hell has this happened?

Sylvia   He asked us.

Ray   You. He asked you. I step out for one second, and now we're responsible for a bloody child.

Sylvia   She is an unaccompanied minor. He just asked us to be reassuring.

Ray   How am I supposed to reassure her, when you spend half the time convinced we're going to die –?

Sylvia   Try your best. And her name is Lianne!

Back to STATE 1.

Ray   Her name was Layla, and Layla was also very, very scared of flying.

Sylvia   Not good.

Ray   Nightmare, *nightmare* situation. I'm sat next to a snotty, hyperventilating mess, and the other one is a seven-year-old child.

Sylvia *genuinely laughs.* **Ray** *smiles.*

Ray   Every time she laughs at that.

Sylvia   He's a funny guy.

In the background, we hear the internal sounds of a plane taking off.

Ray   So by the time we get to take-off, people are starting to stare, because those two are having a meltdown on the scale of Chernobyl.

Sylvia   It's bad, because I'm, like, not good, but she is worse and we're just egging each other on, more and more, and it's getting to the point where I might actually have to move, but then, all of a sudden . . . he just starts talking to her about all the lovely things in the sky.

Ray *takes over.*

As he talks the intense sounds of take-off fade into the gentle hum of mid-flight.

Ray   You've got bees and dragonflies, moths, birds. And then, beyond that, clouds and planets and stars and moons, and when you think about it like that, it's really not such a bad place to spend some time.

Beat. They smile at each other, walking closer.

Sylvia   You did say that, didn't you? I'm remembering that right?

Ray   I did.

Sylvia   And it worked. I'd – I'd never seen him with a child, and you don't know until – but you were excellent. And in that moment, I couldn't have loved you any more.

Ray *gently touches her face. They smile. Beat.*

Scene Three

A sudden sound, like a gasp. They both snap around agitated. Beat.

They carry on, initially talking across:

Sylvia   Uh, alright. We both drifted off, couple of hours maybe, and when I wake up, Layla needs the loo. I ask if she wants me to go with her, but she says no. Goes on her own.

Ray   She wakes me up as she bumps past, so there's this moment where it's just us – us, on our honeymoon, starting this next bit of life – and we're just smiling at each other.

They look across, happy smiles and warm light. **Ray** *sighs.*

Ray   But then suddenly you weren't smiling any more.

Sylvia   No. I was distracted by this man who's just appeared behind him. A man I hadn't seen before. And I instantly knew, there was something not right –

Ray *(to us)*   That's a false memory, created to give the illusion of control –

Sylvia   Something really not ok, but at that exact moment, Layla barges past him, back into her seat, and vomits spectacularly into a sick bag.

Ray   Colossal. That bit did happen.

Sylvia   So I've got the man; his smiling face; and a vomiting child, all in front of me. I look down to check Layla is ok, and when I look back up, the man's gone.

The plane noises slowly grow, the lights tighten.

Ray   He races up the cabin –

Sylvia   I hand Layla's sick bag to a passing attendant.

Ray   Goes straight through first class –

Sylvia   Some reports say a steward tried to intercept him –

Ray   But this is almost certainly not true. At best there was a shout before 200 pounds of paranoia and fear –

Sylvia   Anger and hate –

Ray   200 pounds of bad news goes right into the cockpit –

*A smash from one of the entrances as **The Man** enters the stage. He is huge, powerful, coiled.*

Ray *and* **Sylvia** *float in and out of the action.*

The Man *stalks into the middle, looks wildly around and then carries on offstage.*

An area in the centre becomes 'The Controls'.

Sylvia   The co-pilot is off-duty, so the pilot is on shift.

Ray   The black box records a noise from the cockpit –

Sylvia   A scream, a terrified scream –

Ray   Before the pilot begins to radio, 'Mayday, breach, breach!' The first-class steward hears the call and shouts as she runs towards the cockpit –

Sylvia   But her cry is suddenly shut off when the attacker's elbow connects with her nose.

A sudden cracking noise.

Ray   The steward is badly hurt, leaving the man, the controls, and the pilot –

Sylvia   The cockpit is crossed in three easy steps, and suddenly the pilot's radio contact breaks off as two enormous arms lock themselves around his neck.

Ray   Some theories –

Sylvia   Notice his tone here –

Ray   *Some* theories suggest that the choke is indicative of pre-planning –

Sylvia   It is.

Ray   That the style is too effective. But he could've got lucky, or seen it done in a film –

Sylvia   Or rehearsed the best way to shut off oxygen to someone's brain –

Ray   So, the pilot –

Sylvia   Who never gets enough credit – He recognises that what matters are the controls. So even as those arms start to drag his body back, he holds on.

Ray   Which is bad news for us.

Sylvia   I'm in the process of handing over the sickbag, when –

STATE 3.

A sound of groaning metal cuts **Ray** *off as both* **Sylvia** *and* **Ray** *are forced into their seats.*

Ray   What the hell is –?

Sylvia   Oh God, oh my God –!

Ray   It's ok, it's ok –!

STATE 1.

They snap out of it.

Sylvia   As the attacker wrenches back, the pilot hangs on, pulling the plane up and up and up.

Ray   We climb 8,000 feet in 20 seconds. The pressure forces every passenger into their seats, pinning them down.

Sylvia   The attendant next to me leans into the climb, one hand on my armrest, the other, incredibly, still clutching a full sickbag.

She stares across at the imaginary attendant.

Sylvia   She stays there, just staring at me and I do nothing, because she is a symbol of authority and to help her would confirm that something is seriously wrong.

Ray   Anyone know what happens when a plane is angled beyond 15 degrees?

Sylvia   Come on, let's keep this going –

Ray   Past 15 degrees you will experience a massive reduction in lift. Also known as a stall.

Sylvia   The black box records 22 seconds of the pilot choking. Still he holds on.

Ray   But by now our angle has increased way beyond 15 degrees. The pilot finally passes out, and the engines die.

Beat. The engines' noise has been replaced by the whistling of passing air.

They stand, breathing heavily.

Sylvia   Imagine what it's like to be 40,000 feet in the air, and hear nothing but the breeze.

Beat. **Sylvia** *feels the memory flooding back.*

Ray   And we're still not at the bad bit!

Sylvia   We're four hours into a long-haul flight, means none of us are wearing seatbelts. Which is ok when we're climbing –

Ray   But our attacker's not done. Soon as the pilot's fingers slip from the controls, he grabs them and, with the last bit of momentum, throws the nose of the plane down.

The stage begins to alter.

Ray *and* **Sylvia** *detect the change, half in the action, half out.*

Ray   We all feel the change.

Sylvia   The attendant's front leg straightens as the cabin tips forward, still holding onto this sick bag, and for a moment we're level. Things are exactly as they should be, and we could all have gone home . . . But then –

Light spirals around them with a sound of growing speed.

Ray   Christ!

Sylvia   The cabin suddenly becomes a pit, and she falls –

We hear a fading scream that races past them.

Sylvia   I can still see her face, looking back, looking at me –

Ray   That sickbag made it all the way to first class –

Sylvia   And then –

The sound of a heavy weight whooshes past us.

Sylvia   A food trolley flies past, chasing her down what is now a vertical plane. The impact is sickening –

Ray   She doesn't see the impact. But the sudden reversal of pitch and the rush of air through the engines –

Sylvia   Brings them roaring back to life!

The sound of stressed engines blasts out.

Ray   We hurtle towards the ground at 30,000 feet a minute –

Sylvia   And, for a moment, it's like gravity goes.

Sylvia *and* **Ray** *are apart, reaching for each other.*

Sylvia   All three of us shoot to the ceiling –

Ray   We both take a knock, but Layla crumples.

Sylvia   She screams, terrified, desperately trying to get back to her seat, to a seatbelt, to safety. So I act –

Ray   We both do.

Sylvia   I lock my legs around the armrest, my body drifting out into the aisle, into thin air, but my hands are free –

Ray   I'm calling out to Layla, trying to calm her –

Sylvia   I drag her down, pinning her to the seat. Every fibre of my being fighting not to fall –

Ray   I force myself back, reaching for her arms and –

STATE 2.

A moment of calm. **Sylvia** *speaks, not angry, but shocked.*

Sylvia   He put his seatbelt on. While I was hanging, he got back into his seat and took maybe 5 seconds to put it on. 1, 2, 3 . . .

STATE 1.

The noise flies back in.

Ray   I grab the straps as Syl holds her down and 'click' –

Sylvia   She's in.

Ray   I reach out for Sylvia, stretching, but I can see she's just too far –

Sylvia   He's not going to make it. I can feel my weight falling back. I can see him reaching –

Ray (*reaching across to* **Sylvia**)   Grab my arm!

They reach out for each other, straining against the pull.

Sylvia   I know I don't want to fall. But my legs can't hold on and it's just too far –

Ray   Wait –!

She falls.

Scene Four

The stage changes. **Ray** *vanishes, leaving* **Sylvia** *falling through chaos.*

The light spins with her as she hurtles down the cabin until she crashes to a stop.

A strip of light boxes her in. **Sylvia** *lies in it, gasping after the impact.*

STATE 2.

Sylvia   I can see the – the front row of passengers. (*She looks around.*) I've landed in first class and they're just staring at me – but . . .

A distant shout grows.

Sylvia   But . . . I can see something ahead. Something moving . . .

The shout arrives as **Sylvia** *instinctively rolls to another strip of light that opens next to her.*

Sylvia   A body – a human body – crashes into the space next to me. Before I can check if they're alive, bags start raining down.

We hear the thuds.

Sylvia   I crawl along the wall, still facing the front row, until there's nowhere left to go but another drop . . . I look at the faces, begging them to help me, but they're all staring, horrified, at something else, something behind me. I turn my head, looking down into the cockpit . . .

The Man *reappears, standing at 'The Controls'.*

Sylvia   And there he is. A man. The man. He's stood with his back to me, leaning over a seat, and hanging limply out of it is a dead body. The pilot's dead body. He's slumped over, his head hanging at a painful angle, and beyond them is the sea. This black wall of water, hurtling towards us . . .

The sound of speed mixes with roaring water.

Sylvia   It's just too close, and there's not enough time and it made me so, so angry that it was over and that I was alone . . . and then the pilot's head moves.

The light pumps like a heartbeat. The gasping sound returns.

Sylvia *circles behind* **The Man**, *watching him.*

Sylvia   It twitches, slowly coming back to life, which means he is not dead. And if the pilot is not dead, there's a way out. And I wish it wasn't the case, but there's only me here, so . . .

With a shout she falls onto **The Man**'s *back. Her force rolls him from the controls.*

She carries on talking, in between sections of action.

Sylvia   The impact pushes him away, and lands me right in front of the pilot. I can see his mouth twitching, so I grab his face, screaming 'Wake the fuck up and save us!' And his eyes spring open, fully awake, locked on me, just as –

The Man *throws her from the controls and across the stage.* **Sylvia** *stays on the floor as she talks.*

The Man *approaches.*

Sylvia   It was like being hit by a club. Like hurting me was a casual thing. This man kicked me so hard, my face went cold.

The Man *kicks out at her middle,* **Sylvia** *gasps.*

Sylvia   Instinctively I cover up, trying to turn away. And by chance, by complete luck, the point of my elbow lines up with his shin just as –

The Man *kicks out again, then gives a shout.*

Sylvia   I hear this grunt of – of pain. And realise: I've hurt him. I can hurt this man. So before he can think –

She launches herself at **The Man***'s leg, biting every part of him she can.* **Man** *screams, slapping at her head. A quick flurry of action.*

Sylvia *looks past him, straining at the controls.*

Sylvia   I can see the pilot, slowly – so slowly – sitting up. He looks drunk. Like a child in a toy cockpit, but he reaches out a hand, grabbing the yoke, and begins pulling, every millimetre buying us more time –

A flurry of action. **The Man** *tries to dislodge her.*

Sylvia   I'm holding him to me, keeping him away, when everything short-circuits. My arms flop, my eyes – and I realise he's found my temple, and is now deliberately digging his knuckles into the side of my head, until –

The state changes as she slips from **The Man***, who turns back to the controls.*

Sylvia   He strides back to the pilot, ready to rip his hands away, to finish the job, to crash this plane, when –

Ray   Argh!

He flies onto the stage, leaping onto **The Man***'s back with a shout.*

Ray *hangs on as they act out the below, talking rapidly over each other:*

Sylvia   It's Ray! It's my Ray! Dragging the man back, with this snarl, this look of rage and anger–

Ray   No idea what I was doing –

Sylvia   The attacker's trying to shake him off, but –

Ray   I wasn't expecting to meet another human –

Sylvia   He doesn't actually appear to have a plan at all –

Ray I'm not a violent man –

Sylvia I start to see that the snarl of rage and anger is more a look of outright panic.

Ray I'm screaming at her to help me – Syl!

Sylvia So I leap up and run towards them –

Ray Right towards us, no movement – Grab him!

Sylvia He's buying me no time, no distractions –

Ray So he just boots her, straight in the chest with a crunch, back to the floor –

Sylvia Two fractured ribs –

Ray Syl!

Sylvia I can't breathe –

Ray Help!

Sylvia As this man starts reaching back, searching for Ray's throat –

Ray I can't let go, but I can feel him, squeezing – Syl!

And it's over. **The Man** *throws* **Ray** *to the ground before looping his arms around* **Ray**'s *neck.*

Ray Syl! Help me –

He kicks out, but can't get free.

For a second, **Sylvia** *stares, horrified, but doesn't rush forwards. She looks over, towards the cockpit.* **Ray** *gasps out:*

Ray Please, help! Syl!

A micro-beat, before **Sylvia** *races off, leaving* **Ray**.

As he chokes, the light flickers, then out.

Scene Five

Lights snap up. They sit across from each other. **Sylvia** *is unsure,* **Ray** *looks at her.*

STATE 3.

After a beat:

Ray   Syl . . .

Sylvia *is still looking around.*

Ray   Sylvia.

Sylvia   Yeh. Sorry, what?

Ray   Uh . . .

Sylvia   What is it?

Ray   You're bleeding.

Sylvia   Oh.

She touches her face, finding blood in her nose.

Ray   Maybe if you . . .

He demonstrates lightly pinching the bridge of her nose. **Sylvia** *copies.*

Ray   Does it hurt?

Sylvia   Umm . . .

Ray   Stupid question, really.

Sylvia   It sort of all hurts. Hard to tell which bit –

Ray   Yeh.

Beat. **Sylvia** *keeps pinching her nose.*

Ray   Can I get you anything? We could order –

Sylvia   No, no. I'm fine . . .

Ray *looks around.* **Sylvia** *sees.*

Sylvia   What? What's wrong?

Ray   Nothing. Said they were bringing champagne, so . . .

Sylvia   Oh . . . Oh, yeh. A drink would be –

Ray   That's what I'm saying . . .

He can't settle.

Sylvia   Are you alright?

Ray   Yeh.

Sylvia   Sleep well?

Ray   Not that well, no.

Beat.

Ray   Already had a kip on the plane, so . . .

Nothing. **Ray** *decides:*

Ray   That was a joke.

Sylvia   No, I know – It's just, if I laugh . . .

Ray   Right, yeh.

Sylvia (*of her nose*)   Jesus, this won't stop.

Ray   Here, let me . . .

He gently angles her head back. Beat.

Sylvia   I mean, I've heard of nosebleed seats before, but this is ridiculous.

Ray *gives a small, kind laugh.*

Then starts crying.

Sylvia   Oh, Ray. It's ok. We're alright –

Ray   It's just – it's flying out of me –

Sylvia   I know, I know. Look –

She grabs his hand and puts it on her heart.

Sylvia Feel that? Still beating. We're still here, ok? We're alive.

She pulls him closer, kissing his cheek and comforting him. **Ray** *calms, smiles at her.*

Ray Yeh, that's – sorry. We are – We're ok.

They kiss. A champagne cork pops. They jump.

Both Ah!

STATE 1.

The energy changes as they snap back to addressing the audience.

Ray (*to us*) Not the ideal start to a honeymoon.

Sylvia Not the ideal start to anything.

He remembers, clicking.

Ray Layla. We should – They'll want to know what –

Sylvia Oh yeh, fine, broadly. Uh, concussion, some cuts.

Ray Probably a dislike of rollercoasters.

Sylvia Clung to us like a limpet all the way to the hospital, where her mum was waiting.

Ray Didn't even say goodbye.

Sylvia And left us on the getaway of a lifetime.

Ray *claps his hands.*

Ray Now, you might think a hijacking would kill the mood, but at the start it gave a bit of . . .

Sylvia A bit of something.

Ray To be clear: at the start, but still . . .

Sylvia Yeh.

Ray Romance and terror is a . . . spicy mix.

Sylvia Massages, dinner on the beach, petals on the bed –

Ray   And all the time my heart is like, (*rhythmically*) 'You-should-be-dead. You-should-be-dead.'

Sylvia   A constant surge of –

Ray   Best sex of my life.

Sylvia   Not relationship. Life. Said that on the first night. And it was true.

Ray   There was this chord, this energy, coursing through us. Like we needed to be – be –

Sylvia   Close.

Ray   Yes.

Sylvia   Like, locked together, as close as can be –

Ray   And there's only so close you can get before, y'know . . .

Sylvia   They do.

They look across, reliving it. But then:

Ray   But.

Sylvia   But.

Ray   That relief can only last so long. And the truth is, we were both in a very bad way –

Sylvia   You more than me.

Ray   That's just cos a bunch of other passengers were at the same hotel, and every morning they'd grovel in front of her. 'The person who saved us all!'

Sylvia   It's true. I felt like the Pope.

Ray   So I'm starting to sink while she's still floating on this tide of adoration –

Sylvia   No, I just – I felt different. Like I'd become . . . bigger.

She does genuinely seem bigger, next to the quite frantic **Ray**.
He notices.

Sylvia   But you didn't.

Ray   What an insightful point, sweetheart.

Sylvia   Don't be touchy –

Ray   In those first few days, it was all about now. Am I alive now? Are we together now? And that was a very happy place. But eventually you stop thinking about now and start thinking – y'know – . . . What the fuck just happened to me? And those questions build and build –

Sylvia   Until I'm sat there one morning and:

STATE 3.

Ray   Did you leave me?

Beat. **Sylvia** *looks across.*

Sylvia   Uh, just a coffee, thanks . . .

A moment.

Sylvia   Sorry, say again . . .?

Ray   In the cockpit. When he [had me] –

Sylvia   Yeh, I remember –

Ray   I was hanging onto his back. I was shouting for you to help me –

Sylvia   He kicked me away –

Ray   Yes, but after that. You could've come back – But . . . you left me, right?

Micro-beat. **Sylvia** *doesn't want to lie.*

Sylvia   Yes.

Ray   My memory is just a bit –

Sylvia   I went to the pilot.

Ray　Right.

Sylvia　I had to, because, if I didn't, we were all going to die.

Ray　Ok, it's just – in that moment – I *was* dying.

Sylvia　I know. It was horrible. It was –

She gives a tiny sob/gasp. **Ray** *nods.*

Ray　Ok. Alright.

Quick beat.

Sylvia　We would have crashed –

Ray　I know. I understand –

Sylvia　I had to, Ray. Please, tell me you know that.

Ray　I do. It's just hard to . . .

He gestures to his head.

Sylvia　You'd have done the same thing.

Ray　Would I?

Sylvia　Wouldn't you?

Ray　If you'd helped me, then we could have both gone to the pilot –

Sylvia　We were seconds from the ocean. I had to make a decision.

Ray　I don't think I could decide to not help you.

Sylvia　Well, you decided to put your seatbelt on.

Micro-beat.

Ray　What?

Sylvia　When we went up. I was hanging on by my legs, and you were –

Ray　I was helping Layla –

Sylvia   Yes. But before you did, you put your seatbelt on.

Ray   I don't remember doing that.

Sylvia (*kindly*)   You did, Ray. That's why I fell and you were safe.

Ray   I wasn't safe. None of us were –

Sylvia   Safer than me –

Ray   No, we were all heading to the ground at exactly the same speed.

Sylvia *reaches out and takes* **Ray**'s *hand.*

Sylvia   Ok, ok. We both did things up there, but the point is, they worked. We're alive, right?

He recoils.

Ray   Don't do that.

Sylvia   Ray –

Ray   I'm trying to talk about being choked to death and now you're bringing up seatbelts –

Sylvia   Ok, I'm sorry –

Ray   I was trying to get to you. If I'm not held down then I can't reach out –

Sylvia   You're right –

Ray   And now I have to watch every day as these fucking sycophants cheer you on like – yeh, I'm talking about you, Mike – like I didn't do anything, as if what you did is more – more . . .

Sylvia   It's ok –

Ray (*almost nonsensical*)   If I hadn't – I would have done that – but if I hadn't – he would have done to you what he did to me and that . . .

He holds his chest, unable to talk. **Sylvia** *takes his hand again.*

Sylvia   Ok, I'm sorry. I know what you're saying.

Ray *breathes deeply. She kisses his hand.*

Sylvia   We're alive. I love you, I love you. Ok?

He breathes out, nodding.

Ray   This is mad. We should be the happiest people in the world right now.

Sylvia   We are.

Ray   Then why are you covered in bruises?

Sylvia *gives a small laugh.* **Ray** *softens. He looks at her face.*

Ray   I don't remember you being this bad when I found you.

Sylvia   I wasn't.

Ray   Oh.

Quick beat.

Ray   This was –

Sylvia   After you . . . Yeh.

Beat.

Sylvia   If it would make you feel better, we can . . . talk about it?

Ray   Talk about what?

Sylvia   What happened after he . . . You can ask me how it ended.

Ray   I know already. The police told me – We really don't have to.

Sylvia   Right . . . You don't want to. You don't want to ask me how it ended.

The sounds of the plane builds quickly until:

Scene Six

STATE 1.

Ray *looks around.* **Sylvia** *continues to look at him for a moment.*

Ray   Just your average holiday chit-chat.

Sylvia   Mike didn't show his face at the buffet after that –

Ray   Well, fuck Mike.

Sylvia   Lovely guy. Really didn't deserve it –

Ray   I was having a reaction.

Sylvia   Yep.

Ray   You spend your life being told women want a man with feelings, but you get choked by one hijacker . . .

It doesn't get the laugh. He looks around.

Ray   Sorry, forgot where I was.

Sylvia   There was suddenly this split in how we were responding. He started changing –

Ray   Not knowingly –

Sylvia   No –

Ray   But that sense of relief, of joy, was gone. Tried to hold it in, but –

Sylvia   But it was obvious. Every day he got sadder and sadder, until finally, we just went home. Flew home, I should say.

Ray   Three sleeping pills and a drink at the airport. No effect. Nothing –

Sylvia   Still just as tetchy –

Ray   Added to which, everyone knew who we were. It was horrible.

Sylvia   I felt – Wait, really? Did you think it was?

Ray Yeh! People staring at us, gawping. The bruises were still showing. And they're looking at us like – I don't know – like we're bad luck or –

Sylvia I didn't feel that at all.

Ray Syl, come on, you're changing this after the fact –

Sylvia (*ignoring him*) Being at the airport was the first time I realised that what happened to us affected thousands of people. Everyone flying, or who knew someone flying, had built a story in their heads of things going wrong, but our bit of that story is that it doesn't have to end in disaster. And that made people feel good. Feel safe. I loved being that for people.

Quick beat. **Ray** *eye rolls.*

Ray Right, well, it was also around this time that I noticed she was talking to –

Sylvia Oh, was that the time –?

Ray I did notice.

Sylvia You make it sound like I was doing something wrong.

Ray No, but –

Sylvia Journalists started getting in touch with me. The initial coverage was of the attacker, but then someone got a photo of my bruises –

Ray A very grainy pic with her face, nearly blocked by a large, out-of-focus blob –

Sylvia Does this matter?

Ray Yes, because that blob turned out to be *my* head.

Sylvia Right –

Ray Literally not to be focused on.

Sylvia By the time we got back they were stealing my images and waiting at arrivals.

Ray   Where it was suddenly decided that I didn't matter.

Sylvia   And that was when Poirot here began to suspect that the media were talking to me –

Ray   And that you were talking to them.

Quick beat.

Ray   The stories were so right, and so positive, despite what you – . . . that I realised, I deduced, you were talking to them.

Sylvia   Yeh.

Ray   Right. And that really fucking bothered me.

We jump into STATE 3.

Sylvia *is trying to leave.*

Sylvia   Can you just – please give me some space?

Ray   Well, what are they asking you to say?

Sylvia   I don't know. I think they want me to talk about the flight –

Ray (*laughing*)   You think? And did you ask if I could go on too?

Sylvia   I didn't ask anything, they asked me –

Ray   Just you?

Sylvia   Yes.

Ray   Do they even know I exist?

Sylvia   Of course they –

Ray   That I existed there. On the plane.

Sylvia   I'm sure they do.

Quick beat. **Ray** *nods.*

Ray   I get it.

Sylvia   Ray, come on.

Ray   This story has far more legs if it's one woman against the world, rather than two people working together –

Sylvia   Can we not –?

Ray   Are you going to wear your wedding ring?

Quick beat.

Sylvia   What?

Ray   In their fantasy that you did this all on your own, are you also single?

Sylvia   Do you know what you're saying?

Ray   They're saying I don't exist!

Sylvia   What they're saying is that my experience is different to yours –

Ray   What about my experience? Is mine less interesting because it doesn't fit their angle?

Sylvia   There is no angle –

In a faintly hysterical, mock movie-trailer voice.

Ray   One woman, entirely unsupported, does everything right, in a story you're not allowed to question –

Sylvia   I'm going to be late.

Ray   Starring: Her Vanilla Brand of Progressive Politics, and a bestselling soundtrack by You Go Girl –

Sylvia *snaps.*

Sylvia   What is wrong with you?

Beat.

Ray   Just . . . tell them who I am. That I did something. Please. I know they want a simple story for simple people, but you don't have to give it to them.

Sylvia *goes to speak but* **Ray** *changes his mind.*

Sylvia   Ray –

Ray   Actually, don't. Last thing I want is the kids talking about me when I'm not looking.

Sylvia   Are you going back in?

Ray   Yeh. Term starts today.

Beat.

Sylvia   Do you think you're ready to . . .?

Ray *shrugs.*

Ray   Doesn't really matter, does it? I signed a contract –

Sylvia   Ray, I don't think –

Ray   I'll stay if you do.

Sylvia   You shouldn't go in.

Beat. A step closer. **Ray** *exhales.*

Ray   I can't just . . . sit. Couldn't do it on the beach, can't do it here. I need to be moving.

Sylvia   Go for a walk.

Ray   Very funny.

Micro-beat. Another step.

Sylvia   You're still reliving it.

Ray   Please don't go, Syl. I need you here. I need it –

Sylvia (*not angry*)   So you can shout at me?

Ray   No, so that – so that I can feel better. Please. Let someone else do the talking.

Sylvia   I want to talk about it. It makes *me* feel better.

Nearly an eye-roll, instead a step.

Ray   Ok. Ok. Explain that to me.

Sylvia   You need me to explain the urge to share? You got fifty minutes out of your dad dying.

Ray   I shared that stuff because I wanted people to notice me. Is that what you're doing?

Quick beat.

Sylvia   Talking about it, now that it's over, reminds me that it ended. That he is in custody. That it is done.

Ray   Say it in the mirror.

Sylvia   Very funny.

Quick beat.

Sylvia   There were other people on that plane, it might help them too –

Ray   Oh, what, you're leaving me for them?

Sylvia   No –

Ray   Maybe some of those people want to be interviewed themselves –

Sylvia   Oh, Ray, come on –

Ray   Careful, now you're the one shouting.

Sylvia   I'm not. Look at me. I'm calm.

Ray   Lucky you.

She does seem very at ease.

Sylvia   I want to do this, Ray. I need to help myself too.

Beat. A phone buzzes.

Sylvia   Taxi's here.

Ray   Wait.

Sylvia *stops. Turns.*

Ray   You know this will be the first time we've been apart since . . .

Quick beat.

Sylvia *goes to* **Ray** *and they hug, firmly.*

A moment. She kisses him on the cheek as the hug breaks. Her hand trails off his neck.

She smiles, and leaves.

Scene Seven

STATE 2.

Ray *looks around, embarrassed. Deep breath.*

Ray   Turns out, and I can admit this now, that jumping back into a full-time teaching post may have been – may have caused – some additional stress.

He begins to move around the space once more.

Ray   The screaming and the energy, and of course, they knew. Teachers too, the whole school. My first ever day at that place ended with me crying in a toilet, and this day was very similar, except that it happened in the middle of my classroom. Which was quite the spectacle. So, ten minutes later I find myself in the sick room, breathing into a bag. And in the corner is some horrible, mid-morning TV show, which is bizarrely showing a photo of me. Or of us.

Sylvia *appears, smiling warmly and talking to* **Interviewer**, *who is chirpy and kind.*

Ray   And there she is. My wife.

Sylvia (*mid-conversation*)   We didn't really know anything was wrong until we heard screaming.

Interviewer   That must have been terrifying.

Sylvia   It's not what you want to hear.

Another smile.

Ray   Both of them sat on a huge sofa, his best concerned face on, and her, smiling back.

Interviewer   So I think, really, what we all want to know is: Are you ok? How are you?

Sylvia (*laughing*)   I'm alright, thanks. The overall feeling is . . . luck. Or maybe relief.

Interviewer   Luck? Really?

Sylvia   I know that sounds odd, but just to be alive when I so nearly wasn't, it's incredible.

Ray   She wasn't lying. She does look great. Peaceful, at ease . . . God, I hate her.

Interviewer   See, I think, if that had happened to me, I'd be terrified. I'd be too scared to go outside. How are you so . . . together?

Sylvia   Because we're ok. That's the most important thing. It happened, but we're all alive.

Interviewer   I've gotta say, whatever you're taking, they should have it on the NHS.

Sylvia *chuckles warmly.*

Sylvia   Well, I think it's just the knowledge that, in times of crisis, people stand up to help. I never knew I was someone to do that, and it wasn't just me. My husband, the pilot, the cabin crew. We all did something. It might sound strange, but I honestly feel safer and more confident than before.

Ray *smiles grimly.*

Ray (*to us*)   Now, look. I told you there was a bad bit coming, and you've all been very patient. So here goes.

Interviewer   So, you feel no ill will towards the man who did this to you . . .?

Sylvia   No. None.

Interviewer   You don't hate him? Want to go after him?

Sylvia   That would be . . . vindictive. He did something terrible, yes, but he's been detained. That's justice. That's the system working.

Interviewer   So could you forgive him?

Sylvia   Oh . . . maybe, but I don't know. You've put me on the spot! (*Laughing.*)

Interviewer   Yes, sorry, that was silly. But – but – but it is a question that's likely to come up –

Sylvia   Of course –

Interviewer   Especially now he's been released . . .

Beat.

Sylvia   Sorry, what?

Ray   Bingo! There it is.

Sylvia   What do you mean?

Interviewer   Oh God, I'm – the man who hijacked your plane. Just before you came on, he was –

Ray   Released into custody.

Sylvia   He's – he's been –

Ray   The man who was seconds away from ending 398 lives was let go just weeks later. And she found out live on TV.

Sylvia *tries to hold it together.*

Sylvia   Why – sorry – why has he been released?

Ray   The bag I'm breathing into has stopped moving, by the way.

Interviewer   I'm so sorry, I thought you – He was found to be in a state of high paranoia –

Sylvia   By who? Who found that? Sorry.

Interviewer   Uh, doctors at the centre he was being held in –

Sylvia   And where is that? Is he [here] . . .?

Interviewer   I – We don't have that information.

Sylvia   You don't know where he is?

She can't help but glance around. A ringing begins in the background, distorting her thoughts.

Interviewer   Uh . . . Look, why don't we move on to –

Sylvia   Sorry, but what the fuck is going on?

Interviewer (*laughing uneasily*)   Apologies for the language –

Sylvia *raises her head, somehow different.*

Sylvia   Why . . . Why have they let him go?

Interviewer   Perhaps we should leave it there –

Sylvia   No, no, please tell me. Why have they *released* him?

Interviewer *is racing through their notes.* **Ray** *slowly exits.*

Interviewer   I – I suppose his agitation, his paranoia, he – he wasn't himself.

Sylvia   He was someone though, right?

Interviewer   Absolutely we're all someone. But listen, maybe we should talk about one young passenger who's found their inner peace, using ceramics –

Sylvia   No, what I'm saying is, he might not have been feeling himself, but he did it, so why have they –?

Interviewer, *relieved, finds the note.*

Interviewer   They're saying the assailant has no memory of what happened. And, given there's no memory, there is no intent. They say.

Sylvia   He doesn't *remember*?

Interviewer *takes the chance to move on.*

Interviewer   Now, Sylvia, it has been wonderful –

Sylvia   I think there's been a mistake. I was there, I saw him –

Interviewer   Thank you for your time –

Sylvia   No, listen to me! I'm quite scared now, so can you *please* just tell me where he is . . .?

Interviewer   There are security protocols around –

Sylvia   There are protocols for him? For him?

Interviewer   He's a vulnerable person –

Sylvia   He choked my husband, broke my ribs, drove us straight towards the sea –

Interviewer   But all while suffering from a major psychiatric episode –

Sylvia   And that doesn't – sorry – but it doesn't strike you as . . . (*A breath.*) As *very* convenient?

Silence, the ringing holds.

Sylvia   Sorry, I didn't mean –

Interviewer   Medical experts have cleared him for release. I think a lot of our viewers would be really upset to hear you say that –

Sylvia   Well, I – I – I am not a medical expert. But I am the person who looked that man in the eye as he tried to kill me. He could be watching this right now, all because someone who wasn't there has decided there was no intent?! I know what he was trying to do, I know what he wanted, and now he's free. So somebody, *please*, tell me where he is –!

The interview lights slam off as it is shut down:

Scene Eight

Lights back up. The interview has been ended. We are back in STATE 1, but **Sylvia** *seems confused by the sudden change. Looking around she tries to piece together the next steps.*

Sylvia   As I get up I can see all the people in the studio staring at me, so I just – head down and I run. (*She moves.*) I need to get home, get away from where he knows I am, but the tube is too jumpy, too loud, and I can feel my chest closing up with –

She gasps, holding her chest. She backs into a member of the audience, before leaping away.

Sylvia   And I know he is not here now. But he could be. Because every person, every face has some of him in it, hiding, waiting for –

The sound of the plane builds. Shaking panels and alarms. She gasps again.

Sylvia   There's not enough room, and this pressure is squeezing my – (*She gulps air.*) I'm trying to breathe, trying to calm down, but –

Ray *appears, not in STATE 1, staring at her.*

Sylvia   Ray?

Suddenly he's choking, the arms wrapped around his neck, and it becomes clear: they're back on the plane.

Ray   Syl! Help me –

She watches for a moment, horrified, then turns away. The light on **Ray** *dies.*

Sylvia   No, no! I know it's not real, I *know* it's not –

For a moment, it might have worked, but now the arms are reaching out for her too . . .

Her breath comes in bursts as they get closer.

Sylvia   He's not here, he's not here –

The hands reach her neck, shutting off her voice. She's unable to breathe, stuck in terror, but then the ringing sound from the interview returns.

Her expression hardens and she grips the hands, trying to pull them off.

Sylvia   But now . . . I can feel something pushing back. Someone. Someone alive and heavy, fighting this pressure, growing out of my chest.

The hands break off an inch, she breathes.

Sylvia   It's this voice that says, 'I don't fall when I'm pushed! I don't shrink when I'm hit! Look at my arms, look at my nails, look at my teeth!'

She throws the hands off, standing taller, breathing fully.

Sylvia   It pushes out the fear, pushes him away as it fizzes up into my throat, and when there's no more space to be filled, I just crack. And let her in.

The light snap out.

Scene Nine

STATE 2.

A moment of black, until **Ray** *slinks on, embarrassed and aware of the audience. He's waiting for* **Sylvia** *to reappear.*

Ray   You ever said something that you didn't know you thought, right up until it came out?

Sylvia (*off*)   Hello? Ray?

Ray   Maybe you didn't know it was there, but once you've said something, once you've let that thought in . . . you become different.

Sylvia (*off*)   Ray?!

STATE 3.

Sylvia *bursts in.*

They rush together, hugging each other, both nervous and jumpy.

Ray (*same time*)   Oh my God, where have you been? I was going to call the police!

Sylvia (*same time*)   Did you see it? Did you see what they've done with him?

Ray   Are you ok?

Sylvia   Are you?

Ray   I'm – I don't –

Sylvia   I can't really think straight.

Ray   No.

Sylvia   My brain is just [exploding].

Micro-beat.

Sylvia   Have you locked all the –?

Ray   Course.

Sylvia   Doors and windows?

Ray   Yeh.

They hug again.

Ray   Where were you –?

Sylvia   I had, like, a thing – when I left. I think. I couldn't breathe.

Ray   What?!

Sylvia   But I had to get back to you, so I just started running. And this strange – (*She touches her chest.*)

Ray   It's alright. You're here now. It's just us.

Sylvia   I love you so much.

Ray   I love you too. It's ok.

They finish hugging, still inches apart.

Sylvia   Did you see it? Did you watch?

Ray   Yeh.

Sylvia   Go on.

Ray   What?

Sylvia   Did I . . . Did I seem . . .?

Ray (*same time*)   Angry.

Sylvia (*same time*)   Normal?

Ray   Yeh, and normal.

Sylvia   Angry?

Ray   And normal.

Sylvia   Did I seem angry? I didn't mean to – I wasn't – but then he was just saying these things and – and – Christ – I think I might have come across as some sort of mouth-foaming, lock-'em-up fruitcake –

Ray *hugs her again.*

Ray   You seemed really in control. Really reasonable. I would have – God . . .

Sylvia   Why did they do that?

Ray   I think they were looking to get a reaction out of you –

Sylvia   No, I mean why have they released him? No one would say.

Micro-beat.

Ray   I heard the same as you. He was having a psychotic episode. Doesn't even remember doing it –

Sylvia (*sudden*)   I'm sorry.

Ray   Why? What?

Sylvia   You've been worse than I have. You've been angry, rightly angry. And I didn't listen –

Ray   No –

Sylvia   But I get it now. I feel it too –

Ray   I'm not angry anymore. Honestly. I'm ok.

He hugs her.

Sylvia   He could have been wrong. The presenter, maybe he was –

Ray   No, he's really out.

Sylvia *breathes shakily.*

Sylvia   We need to think about what happened. What actually happened.

Ray   Sure –

Sylvia   Shh!

They look around for a noise, close together.

The moment passes. **Sylvia** *continues:*

Sylvia (*quietly*)   Do you think, like – and bear with me here, but – maybe he got to someone?

Ray   Sorry?

Sylvia   I'm trying to work out how this happens. Does he know someone, or . . .?

Ray *winces, moving away.*

Sylvia   What? Don't laugh, Ray.

Ray   I'm not. But that is a bit far-fetched, no? Sounds like a conspiracy –

Sylvia   A man smashes his way into a cockpit, attempts to kill hundreds of people and then goes free? *That's* far-fetched, *that* sounds like a conspiracy. And all because, what, he thought he was being followed by the CIA?

Ray   There were aliens in the hold.

Beat.

Sylvia   What?

Ray   Apparently he thought there were aliens in the hold, and if we landed they would be released.

Sylvia *snorts.*

Ray   Now who's laughing?

Sylvia   Who told you that?

Ray   It's in the groups with the other passengers, they're sharing articles –

Sylvia   What would they know?

Ray   Makes sense though, doesn't it?

Sylvia   No! Aliens in the hold does not make sense –

Ray   I don't mean – I'm saying it explains how desperate he was! You would be too, if you thought you had to save people from –

Sylvia   Oh my God.

Ray   What? What?

Sylvia   You believe them. You've convinced yourself that he didn't mean it –

Ray (*angry*)   Sylvia, I was with you, I know he meant it!

Sylvia   Sorry, I'm sorry.

Ray   We need to calm down –

Sylvia   I can't! He tried to kill us and now he's out there, he could be looking for us right now –

A knock.

They jump. **Sylvia** *holds* **Ray**'s *mouth shut.*

Another knock.

They wait, not knowing what to do.

Ray   Syl –

Sylvia   Shh! He'll go away.

Ray   The lights are on. He's heard us talking.

Sylvia   Oh God, oh God –

Another knock. Beat.

Ray   I'm going –

Sylvia   Wait, please –!

Ray   I'm not hiding in my own fucking home.

He goes out. Not fully committed.

Pause. **Sylvia** *stares at the exit, terrified.*

The sounds of the plane drifts back as the light tightens.

The Man *walks in. Huge and calm.*

Sylvia *backs away, ready. The sound vanishes.*

Man   Hello.

Beat.

Sylvia   You.

Man   Oh, you remember me.

Sylvia *nods.*

Man   I thought, with all the chaos, you might have forgotten my face.

Sylvia's *breath comes in bursts. Undecided if she wants to fight or run.*

Sylvia   Where's my husband?

Man   Maybe you should sit down.

Ray *wanders in behind* **The Man**, *seemingly unconcerned.*

Ray   Syl, you remember Layla's dad.

Man   Al. Good to see you again.

Beat as **Sylvia** *realises she is talking to* **Al** *and not* **The Man**. **Al** *is aware he's thrown her.*

In this environment, the actor doesn't look quite as big, not as aggressive. It takes her a moment to believe it's someone else.

Ray   Syl?

Al   Perhaps I should come back another time . . .

Sylvia   No, no. I just couldn't place you, was all.

Al   That's alright, you've had a fair bit on your plate.

Little laughs.

Ray   Al was looking for some help with Layla.

Sylvia   Really?

Al   Yes, but before I say anything . . .

He clears his throat, holding back a bit of emotion.

Al   I wanted to thank you. When I asked you to keep an eye on Layla, I had no idea what that would mean, and you helped her when I couldn't. I can't tell you what that means to me.

Ray   Our pleasure. She's a wonderful kid.

Sylvia   Is she alright?

Al   It's been difficult since she got back, and then with . . . that man being released . . .

Sylvia   Sure.

Al   But, I am determined that she sees some positives in this.

Ray   Yeh, great.

Al   Which actually leads me to my next point.

Again, he sets himself, as if nervous.

Al   After the news today, a group of other passengers contacted me about a group litigation order. I know a little of that world, and how difficult it can be, so I – I volunteered myself, on behalf of Layla, to act as the lead claimant.

Ray   You're taking legal action?

Al   Absolutely. And I know that can feel daunting, but I don't want it to be for you – sorry, I practised this so many times: In order to thank you for saving Layla, I would like to add you to the list of claimants and cover all your expenses. I don't want you to raise a finger.

Beat.

Ray   Blimey, Al, that's –

Sylvia   Incredibly generous –

Al   It's the least I can do.

Ray   Well . . . thank you.

Al   No, thank you. Can I take that as a yes?

Sylvia *and* **Ray** *look at each other with a 'why not?' shrug.*

Sylvia   Well, is there nothing we can do to help? I mean, what's the process.

Al   There's very little for you to do. I think there's a strong case of gross negligence to be made against the airline. I'd expect a formal apology, compensation and then aftercare –

Sylvia   Sorry, wait, wait. You're – you're suing the airline?

Al   Yes, of course.

Sylvia   Why?

Quick beat.

Al   People were let down. People suffered.

Sylvia   Yeh, but . . . because of the hijacker. He's the one you should be going after. Surely.

Al   If Layla's school had an unstable pupil who was then allowed to attack her, it's the school who made the mistake. I wouldn't sue the student, that'd be cruel.

Sylvia   Sure, but if I get in a cab and get robbed at the lights, I wouldn't take the driver to the cleaners.

Al   Look, the airline was the decision maker. It holds all the power in this equation and it utterly failed to keep Layla safe. Where were the security systems? Why was the door breachable? Who allowed him on board?

Sylvia (*still polite*)   And what about the man who *got* on board? Who *breached* the door? What about him?

Al   Well, like you said today, to go after him would be vindictive. What would it achieve?

Micro-beat.

Sylvia   You were watching.

Al   Yes.

Beat. **Ray** *claps his hands.* **Al** *stares a little.*

Ray   So, how is Layla? Hmm? How's she doing? You said she was struggling or . . .?

Al   Oh, how long have you got?

Ray *laughs warmly, dispelling the tension.*

Ray   That bad, eh?

Al   Children bounce, apparently, but I really don't know
how much of that is for me or – I wasn't there, obviously, so
I'm struggling to . . . help with it.

Ray   That's difficult.

Al   She also watched today. The interview.

Sylvia   Ah.

Al   I wouldn't have let her, myself, but kids and phones.
And now she . . .

He heaves a sigh. Rubs his face.

Al   She keeps asking me these questions which I just don't
have any answers to. And it makes me feel like a bad father. I
couldn't protect her at the time and now – it's – it's incredibly
frustrating.

Quick beat.

Sylvia   Try me.

Al   What's that?

Sylvia   The questions she has. Maybe we can help.

Ray   Uh –

Al   Really? No, I'm –

Ray   It has been a long day –

Sylvia   Sure, but it's good to have people around. What's
she asking?

Quick look from **Ray** *to* **Sylvia***. Beat.*

Al   Uh, well, she – she was talking lots about you today. The
release and the interview. I think it was strange.

Sylvia   Strange for us too.

Ray   Very weird.

Al   And now she – God – she feels sure he's coming to hurt her again.

Ray   Oh, that's absolutely not –

Al   No, I know, but that's what she thinks –

Ray   But they're saying he didn't actually want to 'get' anyone. Right? I mean, apparently, he doesn't remember a thing.

Al   Yes, but when I tell her he didn't mean to, she can't understand why he did. So I say it was an accident, but . . .

Ray   Well, maybe not accident. He – he was just . . . imagining things.

Sylvia   Sorry, but if she didn't believe it was an accident, then she's not going to buy that the CIA were following him, or aliens, or anything like that.

Ray   Depends how you frame it. You tell her lots of doctors did lots of tests, and that's what they found.

Al   Maybe . . .

Sylvia   Hmm . . .

Al   What?

Micro-beat.

Sylvia   Well, he could have lied in those tests –

Ray   Syl –

Sylvia   But that's what she'll say, right?

Al   Then I'll explain to her: people don't tend to lie about these things.

Sylvia (*with a chuckle*)   Men don't lie about attacking women?

Al (*matching the tone*) People don't lie about being psychotic. If someone says they're ill, they probably are. (*Micro-beat.*) Besides, I think it's best to stay away from any idea he might be lying.

Sylvia Why?

Al Because she's a child. Because the lessons she takes from this will shape her for the rest of her life, and I don't want her believing that people are dishonest.

Sylvia But . . . they can be. People do lie. Has she never pulled a sickie? A sudden stomach ache when it suits her? (*She points to* **Ray**.) He does it all the time to avoid work. I think she knows people can be dishonest.

Quick beat. **Ray** *begins wrapping up.* **Sylvia**, *confused, can't work out whats's going on.*

Ray Food for thought.

He moves **Al** *towards the door.*

Al Sorry, I shouldn't have –

Ray It's just been a long day. We'll let you know if we have any questions.

Al Of course. And if you change your mind about joining us, then my offer always stands.

Ray Thanks.

Al *is at the door when* **Sylvia** *adds:*

Sylvia If you think Layla would benefit from talking with someone else, then bring her over anytime. I'm always happy to see her.

Beat. **Al** *smiles politely.*

Al (*sincere*) Thank you.

He's on the verge of leaving, then turns, unable to hold it in.

Al   Sorry – I would *love* for Layla to talk with you, Sylvia. I think it would do her a world of good. I wasn't there and it's important that she can [share] . . .

Sylvia   Of course, yeh –

Al   But, when you do, if you could be . . . careful with your language, that would be appreciated.

Beat.

Ray   Uh –

Sylvia   Excuse me?

Al   Obviously, it's not my business, I'm not telling you what to do –

Sylvia   Course not –

Al   But I think the way you've described him today, as a brute and a criminal, while contradicting medical opinion. It's unhelpful and damaging. She's still trying to make sense of it.

Ray *tries to get* **Al** *out.*

Ray   Sure, we'll keep that in mind.

Sylvia (*louder*)   I'm still trying to make sense of it.

Al *turns again.*

Al   Right. Of course.

Sylvia   And, as you so obviously pointed out, you weren't there and I very much was.

She cuts **Al** *off.*

Sylvia   And in my experience, attempting to infantalise how someone feels is incredibly unhelpful and damaging, and is an opinion no one needs.

Ray   Let's calm this down –

Al   I don't think I'm being unreasonable: Don't talk to my child in such a reactive way. That's all I'm asking.

Sylvia   Reactive?

Al   Yes.

Sylvia   Which part, specifically, would you say has been –?

Al   The language you use, the narrative, you're looking for a 'bad man', and that's fine for a film, but it's dangerous in the real world –

Ray   He tried to kill your daughter, Al, does that not make him a bad guy?

Al   No, because if you have 'baddies' you need 'goodies' and I'm trying to teach her that life is not that simple. Humans are both, and people who see the world as good or bad are usually idiots –

Sylvia   Wow, Ray, I thought we did a pretty good thing. I had no idea that stopping someone crashing a plane was morally complicated, or am I an idiot?

Al   Well, you damaged him for life –

Sylvia   He was trying to kill us! And he damaged me too. Do you need to see the photos –?

Al   He is an unwell man! You defended yourself, fine. I'm glad you did. But what happened to him is punishment enough, and it does not give you the right to publicly decide he's guilty.

Sylvia   You've decided that he's not! Why are you and all the rest of these people, who weren't there, so determined to believe one report that say he's not responsible?

Al   Because no one serious thinks he's lying!

Sylvia   Well, I do. I saw him with my own eyes, had his hands around my throat, and I'm telling you he *is* guilty.

Beat. The focus falls to **Ray**.

Sylvia   Right?

Pause.

Ray   I – I don't – I don't know anymore.

A horrible silence.

Al *looks for something to say.*

Al   Sorry, I just remembered, it was your honeymoon.

Ray *(quietly)*   Yeh, that's right.

Al *can't help himself:*

Al   How was it?

Sylvia   Best sex of his life, apparently.

Al   Christ.

Sylvia   Don't worry, I won't mention that to Layla either.

Al   I was just asking for a bit of nuance.

Sylvia   Yeh? Well, I'm asking you to [fuck off] –

Ray *(firmly)*   Al, can you . . .?

Al *nods and goes.* **Ray** *watches* **Sylvia**.

Ray   What a prick, eh? What an absolute . . .

Sylvia *can't meet his eye.*

Ray   Syl? Come on. Look at me.

She looks up slowly.

Sylvia   Do you think I'm insane? Do you?

Ray   What? No.

Sylvia   He does. He thinks I've lost it, and all you could say was 'we'll keep that in mind'.

Ray   I was trying to get him to leave.

Sylvia   But do you think I'm wrong?

Ray I think he's making up for the fact he couldn't help Layla –

Sylvia Ray!

Ray I don't think you're insane, or wrong.

Sylvia But you also don't think he's lying?

Ray I don't know, Syl. I really just – I have no idea!

Beat. **Sylvia** *stares as if seeing something for the first time.*

Sylvia You weren't there.

Ray What? Course I was.

Sylvia Not really. That's why you're not sure.

Ray Syl, I was right there, right next to you when –

Sylvia So how did it end? Hmm?

Silence.

Sylvia You don't know, because you weren't *really* there. The only person who was is that lying snake saying he has no memory of it. And he's conned all of you.

Ray This is the kind of language that Al thinks is –

Sylvia I don't care! I don't care what Al, or you, or anyone thinks. I don't chose to feel scared, terrified, under attack, but I *know* I am. Same way an animal knows it's being watched. There is a danger out there, and *none* of you can see it! I know this is true. Question is: do you?

Quick beat.

Sylvia Do you?

Quick beat.

NOTE: Of the below, however many feel right to create **Ray***'s outburst.*

Sylvia Do – do you? Do you? Do you? Ray. Do you? Do you?

Scene Ten

*We snap into STATE 2, with **Ray**'s bottled frustration suddenly coming out.*

Ray Six months of that. Six months of every little anything getting picked apart for meaning. Someone offers us a seat: Do they recognise us? Agree with us? Hate us –

Sylvia *cuts in, jarring us into STATE 1.*

Sylvia For six months, I could barely –

Ray No! Sorry I just need to –

He claps his hands pushing us back into STATE 2. He continues:

Ray A look from a stranger, a cup of tea too hot, someone being difficult at work: For us, against us? Do they, don't they? Do you see that? Do you, do you, do you?!

He moves.

Ray One doctor makes one decision, miles away, and suddenly there's a different person sleeping next to me at night. A person living in smaller and smaller worlds of who *really* understands, which is, of course, no one. Not even me. So I'm starting to wonder if this change is something she can come back from, or if what happened created a chemical shift in my wife –

Sylvia *comes into the light.*

Sylvia That disgusting group won.

*Beat. **Sylvia** is confused.*

Sylvia Sorry, were you . . .?

Ray No, no. You go ahead. Al's group won against the airline.

Sylvia It was a fight at first but the reputational damage became an issue.

Ray Few months later they settled.

Sylvia   Which we disagreed with, obviously.

Ray   Obviously. But in an attempt to save the company name, they made an offer to all affected passengers –

Sylvia   Even the ones at the back who just had a bit of turbulence –

Ray   So, one day we get an £8,000 cheque and free flights to anywhere in the world. Pretty nice of them. The tickets, the cheque are right there in front of me, she's looking at them, I'm expecting a nod, a smile, an anything, but instead she just says:

We snap into STATE 3.

Sylvia   I'm going to quit my job.

Ray *blinks.*

Ray   With eight grand?

Sylvia   Yeh.

Ray   That's not a lot of money, Syl –

Sylvia   To most people that's a lot of money –

Ray   Jesus Christ – Eight grand is *not* enough money to quit your job with –

Sylvia   But I'm not doing my job. I go in, I stare at the screen, but I'm not there. I'm not anywhere –

Micro-beat.

Ray   I know. I'm not blind. But – look, we might not agree with this decision, but at least one's been made. Hundreds of other people think this is what justice looks like –

Sylvia   Well, they're wrong.

Ray   Right . . . I guess I was just hoping you wouldn't see it that way. That maybe it would give us a chance to move on but –

Sylvia   I've ruined it.

Quick beat.

Ray   No. You haven't ruined anything . . . But you keep cutting yourself off, and it makes you so angry, so alone. I don't know why you do it –

Sylvia   I know I'm not myself anymore. I know I'm not. I know you know I'm not.

Ray   Jesus, Syl. That's the saddest thing I've ever heard.

Sylvia   I used to meet someone and I could tell what they were feeling. I had space for other things, other people . . . But now all I've got room for is him.

Ray *nods.*

Sylvia   Please can you tell me how you got better? Please. Because at the beginning you were the worst version of yourself, and now you can walk around like nothing happened.

Ray   That's not how I feel.

Sylvia   So how do you do it? Because either you are repressing this . . . heat, or I've missed how you can just get on with your day knowing he's out there. Please tell me, because it feels like you've left me behind.

Ray *hugs her.*

Ray   Oh, God, no I –

Sylvia   Not deliberately –

Ray   I'm not leaving you anywhere, Syl. I love you –

Sylvia   I know –

Ray   I've just found a different way of seeing it –

Sylvia   But what way? What is it?

Ray   It's hard to explain –

Sylvia   Because it's like I'm screaming 'Fire!', and everyone's just – just telling me –

Ray   Not to say it in front of their kids?

Sylvia *gives a snotty laugh.*

Sylvia   Worse, they're telling me fire doesn't exist, when we're both covered in ash.

Ray *nods.*

Sylvia   He is responsible, he is guilty and he is free to do anything to us. Which part of that equation have you changed to make it work for you?

She grabs his hands.

Sylvia   Please tell me. I want to be me again.

Ray   Maybe there's another way to see it.

Sylvia   In that he didn't mean it? He doesn't remember?

Ray (*not quite believing*)   It's possible.

Beat.

Sylvia   He choked you, until your brain shut off.

Ray   I remember.

Sylvia   So how can you . . .?

Ray *tries to get his thoughts straight.*

Ray   What I know is that between those two worlds, one where he tried to kill me, got away with it and is now on the loose – the world with a fire in it – and the one where a very sad and unwell man made a massive mistake that will never happen again . . . I choose this [the second] one. Because here [first] I can't sleep, I can't breathe, and I don't like who I've become. So –

Sylvia   That sounds like a delusion. He was the one who decided we had no choice in this –

Ray   We do. That's all we have. This is about the person you choose to be once something terrible has happened. And that *is* up to you –

Sylvia   And what about other people? What about your responsibility to shout about the injustice? To make a noise about it.

Ray   You want me to go screaming at every airport in the world?

Sylvia   No, but say I'm right, say he does it again and this time there's no – how will you feel?

Ray   Awful. But I can't live my life under the belief that the worst is just about to happen.

Sylvia   But it did happen, to me –

Ray   To us –

Sylvia   And it will happen again. I have to speak out about that –

Ray   But you don't really mean speaking out. You're not petitioning to change flight rules. You mean getting everyone else to feel as scared as you are and that's . . . wrong.

Sylvia   Wow.

Ray   Sorry, I don't just mean you, cos it's everywhere. Our whole world is full of people trying to do that. When they're panicked the only way they can feel calm is by making other people as terrified as they are.

Sylvia *heaves a breath.*

Ray   I know that belief that the world is trying to get you –

Sylvia   Do you?

Ray   Yes. I've felt it. But there's nothing good down there and it's *not* who you are.

Sylvia *pulls her hands away, moving back.*

Sylvia   It might be. Maybe that's who I am now –

Ray   It's not. The person who walked up to me at that party –

Sylvia   I don't remember that person –

Ray   That's ok, because I do. I remember every inch of her.

He has moved towards her. Sinking to his knees and holding her waist.

Sylvia *holds his head, her eyes shut, trying.*

Sylvia   Oh God –

Ray   The person who told me I couldn't think the world was unfair. Didn't want to know me if I thought things were against me . . .

Sylvia   I want to. I want to feel like her again –

Ray   Then choose to. If you want to bury that man so far behind us . . . Then do it.

She heaves a breath . . . and finally, she nods.

Sylvia   Ok. Ok.

Ray *lifts her up. They kiss. Smile. Pause.*

Ray   So look, if we're after a change, then maybe we start with a change of scenery? And we've got these tickets . . .

STATE 2.

Sylvia *looks out.*

Sylvia   That was his solution: Get back on a plane.

Straight into:

Scene Eleven

STATE 1.

Sylvia *pushes him away, furiously moving around the stage.* **Ray** *reacts.*

Ray   Right, this is where you can all see what I'm dealing with –

Sylvia   I tried hypnotherapy, medication, two different therapists, but Dr Dickhead over there reckoned I just need to get back on the horse, or he's not happy.

Ray   I never said that. You've twisted my –

Sylvia   'The woman I knew' – He's suggesting if I don't get past it then he's gone –

Ray   That's your reading of it –

Sylvia   And what kind of stiff-upper-lip madness made you think getting back on a plane was a good idea?

Ray   Yeh, in retrospect, unwise.

Sylvia   Fucking moronic I would say. We all would say.

Ray   We'd already flown once, I could never have guessed how she would react –

Sylvia   Yes, not having a medical degree he failed to see that a flight to Athens might trigger some feelings!

Ray   I was trying to help you –!

The lights change, the sound of people drifts in as we enter the airport.

Sylvia   Help? Second we got to the airport I was right back to it –

Ray   So was I.

Sylvia   Well, as usual, you managed to choke it down into that cancerous lump in your stomach –

Ray   I forgot that anything less than full-volume emotional incontinence is toxic repression –

Sylvia   From the moment we arrived I'm in bits, but he's walking around, whistling. Whistling in an airport, shopping, people thought he was demented –

Ray   This is ridiculous –

Sylvia   Browsing the classics. The man bought a book –!

Ray   Yeh, *Cuckoo's Nest*. I was looking for inspiration –

Sylvia   Oh, the failed stand-up strikes again!

Ray   Do I need to be here for any of this?

We snap into STATE 3.

Sylvia   I can't.

Ray   Sorry?

Sylvia   I can't.

A Tannoy creeps in, announcing a flight.

Ray   What do you mean?

Sylvia   I cannot get on that plane.

Ray *has an embarrassed look around.*

Ray   Yes, you can. I'm getting on.

Sylvia   I can't.

Ray   Yes you – Look, this is a speed bump, you've just got to run at it, run at the plane –

Sylvia   I'm. Not. Getting. On.

Another look around.

Ray   Syl, I know it's hard, but doing this here, now, is a bit ridiculous –

Sylvia   Ridiculous?

Ray   We've paid for the house, the shuttle, the journey –

Sylvia   Insurance.

Ray   Does not cover having a wobble at the gate.

Sylvia   This is about money?

Ray   This is about moving on with our lives.

Sylvia   Why?

Ray   Because currently I can operate as a human and you can't, so this doesn't work!

Sylvia   He could be on this plane.

Ray *flinches, instinctively darting a look over his shoulder. Quick beat.*

Ray   He's not.

Sylvia   He could be.

Ray   No.

Sylvia   He could be waiting, just through there, ready to snuff you out like –

She clicks in his face. **Ray** *lashes out at the sound, just missing her hand.*

Ray   Stop it!

Moment where neither can work out if he just tried to hit her or not.

Ray   You are giving in to the worst kind of paranoia, indulging it –

Sylvia   I don't care. I am not –

Ray   Come on.

Sylvia   No.

Ray   Come here.

Sylvia   No!

He goes to grab her, she jumps back.

They both feel the escalation.

Ray   He is not hiding, he is not waiting for me. He is in some facility, in the middle of nowhere, drooling into his soup. You get that?

She doesn't move. **Ray** *looks back at the gate.*

Ray   Let me be clear: I am getting on that plane, I am going on this holiday. I will not live a little, scared life.

Beat. **Sylvia** *speaks softly.*

Sylvia   I can't.

Ray   I have to, Syl. I *have* to.

Sylvia   I . . . can't.

Beat. He's about to go to her . . .

Sylvia   Ray, please –

But, instead, he leaves.

Sylvia   Ray!

Scene Twelve

The light gently broadens out into STATE 2.

Ray *looks around, noticing us.*

Ray   I got on the plane. And anyone here thinking that was wrong can . . . I *begged* her to stay when I needed her, I begged . . . So I got on, and I sat by the window, which was my way of saying, 'I am not scared. I will not let this man have a hold on me!'

The light warms.

Ray   And I had a fantastic time. Cried like a baby on the flight, but – it was great. It was like getting half my brain back. I saw the sights, went out, met people, normal people who thought I was normal. Didn't have someone drag every conversation back to the same fucking story –

He checks himself.

Ray   And when you talk to people, without . . . that, you can see: everyone's struggling with something. Everyone. Because, and let's admit this, the toast *does* fall that way. So people need a break because their mum died, or they're lonely, or their life isn't going how they wanted. (*Beat.*) The threat of death, the fear of loss, the unfairness of everything. It's always there, and *yet* . . . we carry on.

The light begins to tighten around him.

Ray   And when I saw it like that, I realised that someone taking over a plane and trying to kill you is really not the worst thing. And as that thought got clearer, this sentence started forming in my head, thumping away like a pulse.

He sets himself:

Ray   'A plane fell out of the sky, and I happened to be on it' – 'A plane fell out of the sky, and I happened to be on it' . . . That's all it was. It's barely worth saying, and I thought I'd be very happy if I never mentioned it again.

A moment.

Unseen **Sylvia** *enters. She's in another scene, not hearing him, but looking for someone else.* **Ray** *is unaware of this change.*

Ray   But, of course, that won't work for us. It can't, because while I need to get away from it, she needs someone who can confirm that what happened, happened only to her. And the cruelty of that, is that no one can do it. If my experience doesn't count, and I was right there with her, then who's left? Who was there?

Sylvia   Hello?

Ray *responds. As he does, the actor who played* **The Man** *and* **Al** *enters behind him, staring at* **Sylvia**. *He is now playing* **Sam**.

Ray   Yeh, sorry. So, by the time I got back –

Sylvia   Hello?

Sam   Hi.

Ray *looks around, confused and unseen.*

Ray   Uh, sorry, I don't remember this happening –

Sylvia *sees* **Sam**. *She's unsure.*

Sylvia   Oh.

Sam   Hello.

Ray, *unseen, looks between them.*

Ray   I don't know if this – I'm not sure –

Sam   Ms Lynn, right? You're Sylvia Lynn.

Sylvia   Uh, yes that's me.

Sam   Excellent.

Ray *watches the scene, eventually fading off.*

Sylvia *and* **Sam** *stand apart.* **Sam** *beams.*

Sam   Uh . . .

He offers his hand, laughing at the strangeness.

Sylvia *laughs too. She goes to shake.* **Sam** *wrings her hands with both of his; after a moment* **Sylvia** *does likewise. They continue to beam at each other.* **Sam** *brings his head down to touch her hands,* **Sylvia** *places her left hand on the back of his head, comforting him. And then they're hugging. A deeply intense and fond embrace that lasts for seconds.*

Sam   It is so good to see you, Sylvia.

Sylvia   You too. I – I don't know what – should I be calling you Captain Howell?

He laughs.

Sam   Just Sam is fine.

Beat. **Sam** *puts his hands on her shoulders.*

Sam   'Wake the fuck up and save us!'

Sylvia   Oh, you remember that, do you?

Sam   The most dramatic alarm of my life.

Sylvia   Yeh, sorry about that.

Sam   Sylvia, you don't ever have to be sorry about anything. You saved our lives.

Sylvia   Well . . . thank you for coming, Sam.

Sam   No, thank you. I wondered if – if you'd ever . . . And I didn't get to say it at the time.

Sylvia   You were busy.

Sam   I was, wasn't I? We both were.

Beat. They smile.

Sam   How are you?

Sylvia   Fine. Ok. Small scar here (*her eyebrow*) but otherwise . . . You?

Sam   I'm – I'm good, generally. There's some damage to my neck.

Sylvia   My ribs too.

Sam   Yes, I can imagine.

Beat.

Sam   How's your husband?

Sylvia   Great, yeh . . .

She doesn't want to lie.

Sylvia   Actually, I – I think it messed him up a bit. A lot.

She gives an uncomfortable laugh.

Sam   Oh, I'm sorry. (*Beat.*) Can I ask . . .?

Sylvia   Ah, it's . . .

She almost resists telling him, then:

Sylvia   It's just – God – It's like two totally different things happened and we're both just, like, disgusted by the other's version. But his idea basically comes down to pretending it didn't happen.

Sam   Right. Yes.

Beat. **Sam** *decides to share.*

Sam   My son and I are also . . .

Sylvia   Was he [on board]?

Sam   No, but he's read a lot about it and he's becoming one of those . . .

Sylvia   One of what?

Sam   Oh, there are some people who think – or who have doubts about . . .

Sylvia   No.

Sam   Oh, yeh. Sceptics, he would say.

Sylvia   About what? What are they . . .?

Sam   Ah, I don't – I think he feels it's too convenient? Allows more surveillance on air travel. They think maybe it was staged.

Sylvia   What?

Sam   Or encouraged, he would say. Not staged.

Sylvia   But you were there. It happened to you.

Sam   That's what I keep shouting at him, but . . .

Sylvia   Don't you find that so . . . so hateable? Sorry –

Sam No, that's ok –

Sylvia Not your son – But . . . it happened to us. None of these people were –

Sam Yeh.

Sylvia I mean, can't he see the marks on you? Doesn't he watch the news?

Sam Well, to be fair to him, you don't believe everything you see on the news either. Do you?

Quick beat.

Sylvia The interview. You saw it.

Sam Oh, yes. Quite the spectacle.

Sylvia I – they surprised me was all.

Sam *nods a little.* **Sylvia** *can't read it.*

Sam And I notice you weren't one of the claimants. I looked for your name on the list but –

Sylvia God, no. We would never have – Al tried, but he . . .

Sylvia *shakes her head.*

Sam He's a character, isn't he?

A small laugh from **Sylvia**.

Sam Do you still feel like that? Like what you said in the interview?

Sylvia *can't work out where he is on it.*

Sylvia I don't know. Maybe. (*Beat.*) Yes.

Sam *nods seriously.*

Sam Me too.

Sylvia (*relieved*) Really?

Sam Yeh. What he did to us. What that man *did* to us . . .

Sylvia   Agreed, yeh. God, it's – he's guilty. Right?

Sam   Absolutely.

Sylvia   And he might well be [ill] –

Sam   Sure –

Sylvia   But we saw him, I mean, we saw him.

Sam   Exactly. So someone telling us that now he goes free because he was, what –

Sylvia   Worried about aliens?

Sam   Excuse me?

Sylvia   He thought there were aliens. In the hold. Or was it the CIA?

Sam   Hearing the voice of God, I was told.

Sylvia   Right, must have missed that one.

She laughs.

Sam   What?

Sylvia   Sorry, it's just – (*Beat.*) I was honestly starting to think that my brain didn't work, that there was something wrong with me. But then to speak with you . . . (*She laughs again.*) It's like warm water.

Sam   Right, yes: your brain is fine. Your reaction is normal. And all these other people should stop talking.

She exhales. They both laugh.

Sylvia   Can we put that on a T-shirt?

Sam (*shaking his head*)   Aliens in the hold . . .

The chuckling dies out.

Sam   None of it's true, you know.

Sylvia   Oh, sure, I –

Sam   But I mean none of it. Like none.

Quick beat.

Sylvia   Sorry, I don't –

Sam   There's a report. Findings of an investigation they did. Won't be available under FOI for a few years but some colleagues thought I needed to see it.

Sylvia   What does it say?

Sam *is pacing, growing agitated.*

Sam   He'd been acting strange for a long time. Security ignored him, police did nothing, but he was obviously not right. He was asking people where the flight deck was. How many crew? Where they were stationed? He was planning it. So they say he's got no memory, but how can that be if he's gathering information and acting on it? He was doing all this and no one said anything, so when I meet him, he seems like just a normal guy who's a bit stressed – and now they won't even admit that's what he was doing, because one ill man is so much easier to take than a cold-blooded killer!

He tries to calm down.

Sam   He was doing all those things and no one told me. They just left us there to – to die. They left us to die.

He points at **Sylvia**.

Sam   If it wasn't for you. You should get a medal. I'm serious.

The sound of gasping grows slowly. Beat.

Sylvia   I didn't know you met him.

Beat.

Sam   For like ten seconds.

Sylvia   When?

Sam   Before we left. Security were concerned, but they didn't want to do anything, so they brought him to me.

Quick beat.

Sam   And if I don't take him that makes him someone else's problem, another pilot. So it's like 5 seconds, 'Is this guy alright?', they don't tell me anything of what he's been doing, and – and he just looked like a really nervous flier. But now I know. Now I understand.

Beat. His smile fades.

Sylvia   So . . . you let him on?

Sam   Uh . . .

Sylvia   I'm just asking.

Beat. Something changes in **Sam**.

Sam   What? You think you could have spotted him?

Sylvia   I did. I did spot him, soon as we got on –

Sam (*doubtful*)   Really?

Sylvia   Yeh.

Sam   How'd you do that then?

Sylvia   Just got a feeling –

Sam   And did you share this feeling with anyone? Pass it on?

Sylvia   It's not my job to assess a passenger –

Sam   Well, it's not my job either! I'm a pilot. Not a psychologist, not a security guard –

Sylvia   No, but you did get asked if he could fly, and you said yes . . .

Beat. **Sam** *gently shakes.*

Sam   I'm so sorry. I think about it all the time . . . They just told me he was nervous . . . When he first came in I – God . . . I thought, for a moment, he'd come to thank me . . .

Sylvia *looks at* **Sam**, *shaken and diminished.*

Sylvia   Are they going to blame you? I'm just thinking with the lawsuit. It was against the airline but if you made the decision . . .

Sam *looks up, suddenly hate filled. Beat.*

Sam   That Al is like a fucking dog. Way he looks at me, it's like I'm not a person, I'm just a thing to be punished. He's got all the compassion in the world for the hijacker, but he's happy to tear my life apart. I'm just collateral –

Sylvia   So will you be . . . fired or –?

Sam   I don't know. There's a review. Of me, of how I acted.

Sylvia   Oh.

Sam   A bunch of grey men asking me why I didn't break the choke at the weak point of thumb or elbow. As if there's no possible reason why I might have forgotten –

Sylvia   Yeh.

Sam   And they ask me things I can't remember. Why did I elevate to this? Why didn't I radio for X? And all I can say is that every decision can be explained by the only thought I had: 'Keep the controls.' Whatever happens, keep the controls . . .

He gives one stifled sob.

Sam   And I did. I hung on, until . . .

Sylvia   You absolutely did. You did so well.

Sam   I thought I was going to die.

Sylvia   Me too.

Sam   I thought I was going to die. And I didn't let go.

He wipes his eyes.

Sam   But none of it would have mattered if you hadn't . . .

Pause. They both think back.

Sam   When he was choking your husband . . . you came to me instead?

Sylvia   Ray was buying us time.

Sam   But not enough?

Sylvia *shakes her head.*

Sam   You stopped him.

Beat.

Sam   I read about it, but also . . . I heard it.

Beat. They can both still hear the screaming.

Sam   That must stick with you.

Beat. **Sylvia** *slowly nods.*

Sylvia   Yeh.

Beat.

Sam   Listen, I know this is strange, but can I hug you again?

Sylvia   Oh.

Sam   It's just, to have been through that with someone and – you're the only one who knows. Like you said, warm water.

Sylvia   Yeh . . . ok.

They go in for a much more awkward hug than the first. **Sam** *is clearly getting a lot from it. He sobs and laughs at the same time.*

Sam   Y'know, sometimes I feel like the second we started falling they dug this huge grave for everyone on board. But then you showed up when you weren't supposed to, so no bodies.

Sylvia *extricates herself.*

Sam   But the grave's been dug, so now they're trying to put us in it, doesn't matter if we're alive or not.

Sylvia (*polite smile*)   Careful, you sound like your son.

Quick beat.

Sam (*concerned*)   Do I?

Sylvia   No, I'm just –

Sam   Don't say that. Don't say I sound like someone who has no idea what –

Sylvia   Honestly, I wasn't –

Sam   This is exactly what you said was happening. You show someone how you feel, how you really feel, and they tell you it's wrong!

Sylvia   It was just a joke –

Sam   It's how I feel!

Sylvia *turns away.* **Sam** *tries to win her back.*

Sam   Sorry, I'm all over the place.

Sylvia   No, I've upset you. Maybe I should go –

Sam   I know where he is! I know where he is now.

Sylvia *freezes.* **Sam** *revels in the effect.*

Sylvia   How do you –?

Sam   My son found him. It's easy enough if you know where to look.

Beat. The gasping increases.

Sam   Do you want to know? I can tell you.

Sylvia *stares.*

Sylvia   He's in some facility in the middle of nowhere, drooling into his soup –

Sam   Nope. He was released.

Sylvia   I know, but into custody.

Sam   Into the custody of his family, which means *nothing*.

Sylvia *covers her face.*

Sylvia   Tell me that's not true.

Sam   It's all true. Everything you ever thought is true.

The gasping builds.

Sam   When you find out, you'll never sleep easy again –

Sylvia   I know what you're doing. You feel better making other people as scared as you are –

Sam   He's not being watched, he's not being checked. He holed up with Mummy and Daddy –

Sylvia   Don't tell me –

Sam   Ten miles from here.

Sylvia *flinches.*

Sylvia   Shit! I really, really didn't want to know that –

Sam   He's in the city, right now.

Sylvia   I'm trying to feel better –

Sam   No chance of that! You are in *danger*, Sylvia. So long as he is out there. It would take him two minutes to find out exactly where we are. Can you live the rest of your life with one eye on the door and one trying to see who's over your shoulder –?!

Sylvia   Please, just stop talking!

Sam   You hurt him once. Maybe we could hurt him again

. . .

Quick beat.

Sylvia   I – I need to leave.

Sam   No, don't –

Sylvia   I'm trying not to think like this –

Sam   What, like you're in the real world?

Sylvia   I just – I'm going.

Sam   Can I have another hug?

Quick beat.

Sylvia   No.

Sam   Please, the rest of the time I feel so scared, but with you . . .

Sylvia   I don't want –

He's moving forwards.

The lights begin to change as she forces the story into a different state.

Sam   Sylvia, listen to me –

Sylvia   No!

*She pushes **Sam** away. The lights change as she runs out of that scene, into a new one.*

Sam *exits.* **Sylvia** *moves into the middle as* **Ray** *reappears.*

*He tries to take the scene into STATE 1, but **Sylvia** refuses, desperate to act out her thought process in STATE 3:*

Scene Thirteen

Ray   Come on.

Sylvia   No.

Ray   Yeh, come on, let's –

Sylvia No.

Ray We've gotta wrap this up.

Micro-beat. Decision:

Sylvia I want to *find* him!

She wins, and the lights return to STATE 3.

Ray *sighs deeply and moves to centre stage.*

Ray (*to us*) Sorry about this.

He turns to **Sylvia**.

Ray Ok. Let's find him.

Sylvia I'm serious.

Ray Me too. Did you really meet the pilot?

Sylvia Stop. I want to – to hurt him.

Ray You already hurt him.

Sylvia I want to do it, Ray! I want to mean it, like he did. I want to find him and punish him for –

Ray Watch out, Liam Neeson.

Sylvia Don't laugh at me.

Ray Going to pull his nails? Attach a battery to his nipples?

Sylvia No, but I – I want him to feel as scared as I am!

Ray You're not that person, Syl. You don't do revenge missions.

Sylvia That man made me like this!

Ray Didn't make me like this. Didn't make 398 other people like that.

Sylvia They didn't have the same experience –

Ray Oh my God, of course they did!

Sylvia   No.

Ray   Listen to me, if you insist on the special, protected, uniqueness of your pain, the individuality of it, then that's what you'll become. Unique, individual, *alone*.

Sylvia   Ask me how it ended.

Ray   Ha!

Sylvia   Come on, if we all had the same experience then you shouldn't have a problem asking –

Ray   I don't feel the need –

Sylvia (*with a cruel laugh*)   Can't do it, can you? You can't bare to ask because you know that what I had to do *was* different, it *was* unique and you will *never* understand it –!

Ray   Oh, shut up!

As he snaps at her the lights come up, back into STATE 1.

Ray   This is what we come back to every time. This loop. You want to find him, want to hurt him, scare him, then no, then you don't want to hurt anyone, then we start again –

Sylvia   That's so easy for you to say. You weren't there –

Ray   Everyone else has moved on. *Everyone.* The hijacker's probably settled down and opened a fucking cafe, and at one point, surely, you'll realise that it's you who's keeping this alive –

Sylvia   I didn't ask to be this person –

Ray   You drag us around and around and there's no end. I cannot live just based on what happened to us.

Sylvia   How can you ignore it? He's not a fiction of my mind. There is a tangible danger that you are desperate to ignore.

Ray   It's not – Christ – A plane fell out of the sky and we happened to be on it, that is all that –

Sylvia   Oh, that is not all that happened. That is such a brainless thought --

Ray   A plane fell out of the sky –

Sylvia   Oh, that so cool, bro. Such a wide perspective. But it's not surprising that you're eager to let it go when all you did was show up, get choked and pass out in your own piss! You left me, and you have *no idea* what I went through –

Ray (*mocking*)   Because I just feel like, for me, when we're talking about me, it's, like, my truth, and my life, it's my me, it's my me me –

Sylvia   Oh, fuck you!

Ray   Yeh, go tweet about it –

Sylvia   I can't be around this, I can't –

She turns away. **Ray** *goes after her.*

Ray   Then stop letting it define you! Please. Just let it go.

Sylvia   It's not a choice! This means something.

Ray   It doesn't.

Sylvia   It does.

Ray   It doesn't.

Sylvia   No, it does! Stop telling me that –

Ray   You could have been hit by a car today, robbed, fallen down, heart attack. All of those things could have happened to you, to everyone, because they did happen, today, to someone else. But they're all at peace with it because –

Sylvia   You think everyone is at peace with it? The arrogance of that is mind-blowing –

Ray   My arrogance? I think it feels good to you. That's why you do it. That's why you keep turning it over and –

Sylvia   What?

Ray   This horrible thing happened to you, only *you*.

Sylvia   You think it feels good?

Ray   I think it feels better than the idea that there is nothing special about us, and no one should care.

Sylvia   I know what this is. You're desperate to make it into nothing because you failed at it.

Ray   Oh right.

Sylvia   You didn't have what it took, natural selection weeded you out, and the only way you can live with that is to pretend that we were just falling and whatever happened was of no –

Ray   We did fall.

Sylvia   You fell, I fought! I became something else up there. I did things and I didn't come down the same person. You have to believe me!

Ray   No one gives a fuck about what happened to us, and they shouldn't have to. You can keep talking about it, string it out, people will call you brave – this lot'll lap it up – but the rest of the world will be cringing at how important you think your life is. And do you know what they'll be thinking whenever you speak? 'When is she going to shut up?'

The Man *appears behind* **Ray***, who doesn't see him.*

He stares across at **Sylvia***, twitching, ready to fight.*

Sylvia *sees him. She kneels on the ground, suddenly exhausted.*

Sylvia   No, no, no. God. I'm so tired. I don't want to feel like this.

Ray   Me neither. Please, Syl, please. I want our life back too. Come with me. We just fell –

Sylvia *can't take her eyes of* **The Man** *but tries to stay in the conversation with* **Ray***.*

Sylvia   No.

Ray   That is all that happened.

Sylvia   It's not – you weren't there.

Ray   I *was*. These things didn't just happen to you. You are not alone –

Sylvia   Your choices were taken from you. I had to make them, had to become them.

Ray   Please, Syl, please.

Sylvia   I – I –

Ray   A plane just fell out of the sky. Let that thought in, let it free you –

The Man *latches his arms around* **Ray**'s *neck.*

STATE 3.

We're are back in the cockpit, the sound of roaring engines and emergency alarms.

Ray *chokes, unable to throw* **The Man** *off, until he goes limp, sliding to the floor.*

The Man *and* **Sylvia** *stand, the controls between them.*

A beat, and then they rush at each other. The fight is horrible and scrappy. There is nothing slick, just two desperate people. Throughout we hear grunts and yelps as they hurt each other.

The Man *is trying to get* **Sylvia** *into a choke. Twice he tries, but she wriggles out. Eventually he drags her to the floor, and tries to wrap his arms around her neck.*

Sylvia *manages to isolate a hand, finding his middle finger. We hear a horrible snap as she bends it sideways.*

The Man *screams, throwing her aside and stumbling towards the controls.*

Sylvia   No!

She rushes towards him, leaping onto his back. She begins attacking his head, trying to get him to let go.

Finally, she reaches around and digs her finger into his eye, trying to pull it out.

The Man *screams and lets go, but* **Sylvia** *holds on, slowly pulling the eyeball out.*

Blood pours from the wound and onto her hands as **The Man** *falls to the floor, howling in pain.*

Ray *stands, returning to his previous spot and carrying on as if nothing had happened.*

The sounds fade away, returning us to the exact point we were at before, except now a bloodied **Sylvia** *stands over* **The Man**, *holding something in her hand.*

Ray   A plane fell out of the sky, and we happened to be on it.

Sylvia *can't stop staring at the bloodied man.*

Ray   You'll feel better, I promise.

Deep sigh, then:

Sylvia   A plane fell out of the sky.

Ray   That's it yeh.

Sylvia   And I happened to be on it.

Ray   We all were. You're not alone.

For the first time **Sylvia** *looks up at* **Ray**, *stares for a moment. She then looks at her hand and what it's holding.*

Ray *finally notices what's happened. Beat.*

Ray   Syl?

Sylvia   Let's go again.

Lights snap off.

The gasping stops.

End.

Discover. Read. Listen. Watch.

A NEW WAY TO ENGAGE WITH PLAYS

This award-winning digital library features over 3,000 playtexts, 400 audio plays, 300 hours of video and 360 scholarly books.

Playtexts published by Methuen Drama, The Arden Shakespeare, Faber & Faber, Playwrights Canada Press, Aurora Metro Books and Nick Hern Books.

Audio Plays from L.A. Theatre Works featuring classic and modern works from the oeuvres of leading American playwrights.

Video collections including films of live performances from the RSC, The Globe and The National Theatre, as well as acting masterclasses and BBC feature films and documentaries.

FIND OUT MORE:
www.dramaonlinelibrary.com • @dramaonlinelib

For a complete listing of
Methuen Drama titles, visit:
www.bloomsbury.com/drama

Follow us on Twitter and keep up to date
with our news and publications
@MethuenDrama